PENGUIN BOOKS

Home Tree Home

# Home Tree Home

**Principles of Treehouse Construction and Other Tall Tales**

Peter Nelson
& Gerry Hadden

PENGUIN
BOOKS

PENGUIN BOOKS
Published by the Penguin Group
Penguin Putnam Inc., 375 Hudson Street,
New York, New York 10014, U.S.A.
Penguin Books Ltd, 27 Wrights Lane,
London W8 5TZ, England
Penguin Books Australia Ltd, Ringwood,
Victoria, Australia
Penguin Books Canada Ltd, 10 Alcorn Avenue,
Toronto, Ontario, Canada M4V 3B2
Penguin Books (N.Z.) Ltd, 182–190 Wairau Road,
Auckland 10, New Zealand

Penguin Books Ltd, Registered Offices:
Harmondsworth, Middlesex, England

First published in Penguin Books 1997

3   5   7   9   10   8   6   4

Line drawings by Peter Nelson

LIBRARY OF CONGRESS CATALOGING IN PUBLICATION DATA

Nelson, Peter.
Home tree home: principles of treehouse construction and other
tall tales/Peter Nelson and Gerry Hadden.
p.    cm.
Includes bibliographical references (p.   ).
ISBN 0 14 02.5998 8 (pbk.)
1. Tree houses.   I. Hadden, Gerry.   II. Title.   TH4885.N45   1997
690'.89—dc21      96–54737

Printed in the United States of America
Set in Electra
Designed by Deborah Kerner

*To our parents*
NORMAN,
SALLY,
SANDY,
AND TRISH

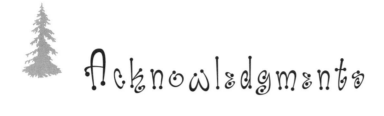

# Acknowledgments

Special thanks to the hardworking crews that helped turn dreams into reality:

GUS GUNTHER'S ALASKA TREEHOUSE—Dave Atcheson, Todd Black, John Bramante, Katie Bramante, Charlie Crane, Melissa Devon, David Fall, Mike Geist, Gus Gunther, Bill Kelly, Sandra Lewis, Tony Lewis, Kathy Riba, and Jason and John.

FOR ALBERT'S MONTANA TREEHOUSE—Albert Green, Ian Jones, Kevin Keeley, Sam Lawrence, John Mackenzie, Tony Martin, Judy Nelson, Cavin Philbin, Emily Philbin, Larkin Philbin, Michael Robb, Kevin Sweeters, Roland Torngren, Sr., and Roland Torngren, Jr.

FOR THE FALL CITY TREEHOUSE—Jake Jacob, Ian Jones, Jamie Lynch, Judy Nelson, Charlie Nelson, Emily Nelson, Henry Nelson, Leigh Turner, and Nicholas White.

Additional thanks for their help and inspiration to: Josh Adam, Jamie Atkeson, Lisa Coffin, Nancy Coffin, Judy Davis, Jan Jahnke, Charlie Kellogg, Gaylord Kellogg, Gary Mackenzie, Kelley Mackenzie,  Ted Mader and Associates, Jeff Marcus, John Moran, John Neilson, Ray Nelson, Herschel Parnes, Hillary Post, Sally Rial, Inga Rouches, John Rouches, John Stevens, Kipp Stroden, Leah Turner, Tim Turner, John Tyler, Uptown Espresso In Seattle, Roger Vergnes, the Wyckoff family,  and Katherine Younger.

Particular thanks to Judy Nelson, Katie Bramante, and Mason March for their photographs.

And a very special thanks to the magical man in the trees, Jonathan Fairoaks, and the treehouse pioneer, Michael Garnier.

# Contents

Home Tree Home

# Introduction

**When was the last time you sat in a tree? Most of us**
are hard-pressed to remember. We recall being in trees at various times in our childhood—whether a few feet off the ground or clinging in the wind to the highest branches—but it's difficult to pinpoint the episode that marked your last climb. How old were you? What changes in your life compelled you to remain thereafter earthbound? The reasons vary, no doubt: school, the opposite sex, a latent fear of heights, physical growth (faster than most trees'), adolescent embarrassment. Whatever the reason, it probably wasn't a milestone you marked off consciously. In retrospect, giving up the trees probably just happened.

As adults, we easily forget peering out from the foliage—feet balanced surely on a swaying branch, hands clutching safety to either side—while we watched our older brother mow the lawn in the distance, or our mother reaching up to hang the laundry on a line far below us and far away, or our sister storming around the house intent on killing us for dressing her Barbie in G.I. Joe fatigues . . .

When did trees become simply lumber, obstructors of our view, or, at best, detached objects of beauty? Like so many aspects of our childhood, the experience seems lost forever.

It is not lost.

You may not be young enough anymore to climb a tree, branch by perilous branch, but so what? The important thing is being in the tree, not how you get up in it. Besides, there are plenty of ways to climb. This book will help you get yourself up there, by whatever means necessary.

Now, you may be visualizing yourself clinging precariously to a limb, pine needles falling in your hair, wondering how to get down and thinking, Forget it—I'll die here. But hold on—that's not what I have in mind. "Tree-being" actually can be quite comfortable. You can bring into the tree all the creature comforts you want: a floor to stand on, a roof to keep the rain off, walls to ward off the wind, even windows, furniture, electricity, plumbing. . . . You can see where this is heading, right? Skyward, into a treehouse. A big one, a small one. A round one, a square one. Eight feet off the ground, or thirty-five feet up. A weekend getaway, a backyard office. Heck, you can move *permanently* off the ground if you want to—into a fully functional, fully rigged treehome. Without giving up any of the luxuries you're used to, you can rid yourself of the endless stretch of stresses associated with ground-dwelling. What you gain is what you thought you'd lost all those years ago as a kid.

*Home Tree Home* sets out in two ways to help you build your own treehouse: First, I'll take you step by step through four illuminating case studies—that is, treehouses I've actually designed and built—from the genesis of the idea through construction; second, I'll discuss in great detail the countless and essential rules of thumb that will save you time, money, headaches, and sprains in your quest for a place off the ground. By the time you finish this book—and I strongly suggest you read the whole thing before you reach for your tools—you'll be armed with the knowledge you'll need to revive that old childhood reality.

Using stories, detailed plans, drawings, and photos, the case studies demonstrate every conceivable technical aspect of building a treehouse. I've also added some of my own unconventional building tricks and hack carpentry techniques to help you out. The book does assume some basic knowledge of simple carpentry, especially tool use. Beyond that, we've laid out all the "special" knowledge for you.

This book is for everybody: for fathers and mothers looking to build a playhouse for their kids; for fathers and mothers looking for a place to *escape* from the kids; for any adventurer who wants a place of his/her own; for anyone, really, with a fanciful inclination. Just remember, anyone can build these structures. I am not a rocket scientist (or whatever its equivalent is in carpentry)—in fact, I refer to myself lovingly as a wood butcher. So put aside your master-carpenter inferiority complex, pick up this book, and strap on your tool belt. Go forth and build safely and well, but remember my motto if you get bogged down in the labyrinth of complex building technique: Done is better. In other words, push on at all costs.

If you've already decided to build—and picked out and approved the tree(s)—I have a final question for you: *If you're going to build a treehouse, why not live there?* It's possible; people are doing it happily and making their friends jealous. That's what this book is all about—the possibilities for happiness. If you make your friends jealous along the way, well, maybe they'll draw their own line and cross to the good side, too.

The treehouses you're about to learn to build all have straightforward designs. And if you have fun building one of them, wait till you hang out in it. If you take your time, you'll end up with a solid structure that you'll flip over every time you see it.

Sometimes at the beginning of a project I see the big picture so clearly in my own head that I can't imagine the work taking more than a few days to complete. But as any carpenter knows, projects almost always take longer than expected, no matter how prepared and efficient you think you are. You've got to remember that each small step takes time and has its own logic. I'm convinced that anyone can be a good carpenter if they just slow down and think about how everything fits together. All of my completed treehouses *look* complicated, but that's the very trick, if you will, of carpentry: the better the work the more you mask the nuts and bolts, the mechanics, of your project. All you can see is the beauty of it.

Now, before I take you into the details of my four treehouse designs, I want to spend a minute on what I believe is the most important theme in this book: openness. You've *got* to be open to the idea of a treehouse or it'll never happen. The following story is about openness, and also about how bizarre and rich life can be. It helps explain the magic and possibilities of treehouses. How Gus Gunther came to live in a tree taught me a lot about how to succeed and how to take advantage of opportunities—opportunities lost on those with closed eyes and closed minds.

## Who Lives in Treehouses?

**G**us Gunther is not normal. In fact he's one of the strangest young men I've ever met. Which, it turns out, makes him a perfect candidate for a treehouse.

Gus and I met in August 1995 while I was in Alaska visiting my childhood

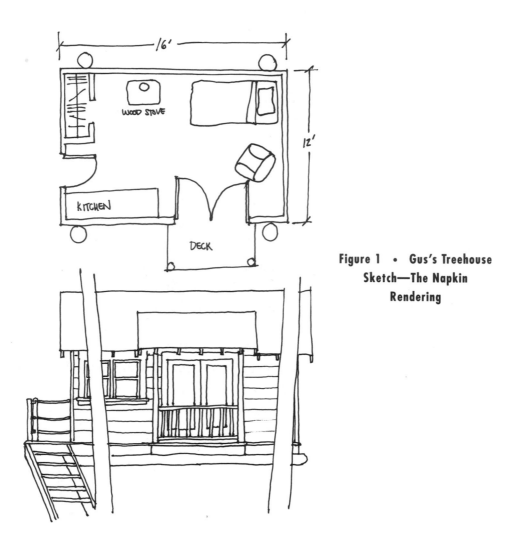

**Figure 1 • Gus's Treehouse Sketch—The Napkin Rendering**

friend John Bramante, now a doctor on the Kenai Peninsula. I'd flown up from Seattle for a long-planned fishing trip on the Russian River, just an hour from John's house. I had no idea when I landed in Anchorage that I was about to meet the future owner of a Pete Nelson Special. But just moments after I arrived at John's house, I heard footsteps coming up the basement stairs—a slow, methodical clumping. The basement door opened slowly.

"Hello to you!" said the disheveled figure before us, a scraggly twentysomething with long blondish hair and a matching beard. He was barefoot, in ripped jeans and a flannel shirt. He was munching on a chunk of smoked salmon. "Name's Gus," he said. "Gus Gunther."

"Hi, Gus," I said.

"Hey, Gus," said John. He turned to me. "Gus is staying in our basement for a little while." Gus and I shook hands.

"Hello to you," he said again.

John and Gus had met by chance playing soccer a year earlier. At the time, twenty-five-year-old Gus was running for mayor of Clam Gulch, population 800. His platform was "No experience in politics." John was talking to one of the opposing players about the elections and laughing at Gus's slogan. That stranger turned out to be Gus (can you say "small town"?). After that they became good friends.

Born and raised in Pennsylvania, Gus found himself in Alaska shortly after finishing college, working as a sports reporter for a small paper. He came to Alaska not looking to drop out of society, like so many others, but in search of a "low impact" lifestyle. After a year of reporting, he quit, citing office politics and bad lighting. He hasn't looked back, or gotten a job indoors, since. Gus isn't exactly a millionaire, but he's getting by on sporadic odd jobs. Currently he's a dog musher and commercial fisherman, and that suits him just fine. One day, during the construction of his treehouse, he smiled at me, happy as a peach. "You know," he said, "I quit the paper fifty-four months ago, and for forty-one of those months I've been on vacation. Not too many companies I know can offer a package like that!"

Gus got into mushing a couple of years back while baby-sitting a friend's dogs. And he discovered he was good at it. In his first Iditarod—the trans-Klondike race from Anchorage to Nome—he finished thirty-second, a very good showing for a rookie. When I first met Gus he was already a deeply committed musher. He'd amassed eighteen sled dogs of his own, trading for them with his own labor, and had more pups on the way. With all those dogs, fishing was barely bringing in enough money to keep his pack this side of healthy. It left almost nothing for Gus, much less money for rent. So there he was, living in John's basement until he could get on his feet.

Problem was, Gus had all his dogs on John's property, and John was getting into trouble with his neighbors over covenant restrictions. In some Alaskan subdivisions they actually write into the deeds that sled dogs cannot be kept on your

The doctor had an interest in seeing the treehouse completed and he proved to be a fast learner.

property. It had reached a head and finally Gus was going to have to leave. But he had nowhere to go.

Enter Pete. One evening just after the fishing trip, Gus, John, and I were playing cards and kicking back, trying to figure out what Gus should do. The obvious idea didn't hit me until a few beers later.

"Wait a sec, Gus," I said. "How would you feel about living in a tree?" His eyes lit up. "What?"

I explained to him what I did for a living, and before we knew it, we had a floor plan drawn out on a napkin. Gus was so excited he said he would head out the next day and put a payment down on some land with his meager savings. It seemed Gus had already had his eye on some property on the road to Homer and God knows there looked to be enough land on the peninsula to go around. I told him I'd return in September or October, once the fishing season had ended and after he had found some land with trees on it. I left Alaska as enthusiastic as Gus, but with many doubts. I mean, here was a guy who'd spent five winters in Alaska—*five winters*—without a home. He'd slept in tents for a couple of seasons, huddling with his dogs for warmth. One year he built a small uninsulated shack out of plywood sheeting—again, huddling with the dogs. In the fifteen months prior to our meeting, he'd lived in fifteen different places. That's a tough feat to pull off anywhere. As Gus put it, "If I tried to do that in Pennsylvania, with eighteen dogs, they'd call Social Services on me." Not so in Alaska.

Gus and I kept in touch through September. Then one day he called to say he'd found the perfect piece of land, and the deal had gone through. Gus Gunther was a landowner. I bought a plane ticket back to the Kenai.

The 12 × 16-foot treehouse was to be Gus's first home. On the flight to Alaska I kept thinking how this huge event was set in motion by chance over a poker game. Six weeks ago, Gus was looking at the prospect of another homeless winter. Now, once we'd finished, his biggest worry would be what color to paint his front door. Yes, I thought, Gus's open and positive attitude, combined with a deep fear of frostbite, was what was making this project possible.

Two weeks later, pounding the last few nails into the roof of Gus's new home, I felt deeply contented. I stopped to rest for a moment, knowing

**It was at this stage that Gus started to think about turning the project into a Bed & Breakfast. After some excited bantering we concluded that Gus wasn't the B&B type.**

**Martha Stewart has nothing on you now, Gus.**

the work was just about done. Below me, in the red glow of the sunset, was a scene I'll never forget: five groups of dogs spread across the long poop-ridden clearing that marked Gus's "front lawn," each doing battle with the other, acting out the complex tribal customs that we bipeds will never understand— barking, snarling, howling, peeing. One lone animal was busily eating someone's camera bag behind a fern. Gus was chasing another with a boot in its mouth. The air was filled with all manner of animal and people chatter. I pulled my hat down over my ears. The temperature was dropping rapidly. I didn't exactly envy Gus's life, but I could see how happy he was. Earlier that day he'd said to me, "Pete, I'm never leaving Alaska. I feel like it was custom built for me. And now I've got a tight little unit to live in." Surveying the scene from his rooftop, I sort of knew what he meant.

# Right Tree, Wrong Tree—
## Picking the Tree to Live In

**Before you start building a treehouse you've got to** ask yourself a whole bunch of questions: How high up do I want my treehouse to be? How will I get up there? How big do I want to build? What sort of view am I after? What direction do I want to face? But I advise not spending too much time firming up details before you've selected your tree(s). Those decisions are actually better left to the tree itself, for this reason: YOUR TREEHOUSE DESIGN DEPENDS ON THE TREE(S) YOU BUILD IN.

A lot of people think it's the other way around—that you can decide on a style of treehouse, then set about finding a tree to accommodate it. It's possible to approach things this way, but, believe me, it's much more difficult. This is true for several reasons. First, you may not have that many trees to choose from. And second, even if you have acres of land to comb for the perfect tree to support your "hexagonal inverted hanging hutch," it may not be in the best location. It might be stuck in a ravine, or have a terrible view, or be too far from a power source or a bathroom or other amenities. And also remember, if you can hardly reach the tree to begin with, you're going to have tons of trouble setting up a work site below it—

---

*Photo at top of page:* **The shape and size of your treehouse are largely determined by the shape and spacing of the host tree or trees. This one on Mercer Island fit snugly into a stand of cedar and fir trees.**

where a lot of the building will necessarily take place. A good rule of thumb is to ask yourself whether you can get close to the tree with a pickup truck. If the answer is no, move on.

What you *can* narrow down before choosing your tree are the more general, abstract, and aesthetic issues: What will I use it for? Is it for me or my kids? Do I want a porch on it? How will I decorate the interior? The answers to these questions have less impact on structural decisions. The important thing is to stay open to changing your idea of the house to fit whatever tree you finally decide on. Like the tree itself, your treehouse plan needs to be flexible. It will probably even change a bit as you're building.

Let me back up and give you some good news. Choosing trees is easier than it seems. So far, the majority of people I have worked with have told me the same thing: One particular tree just jumped out at them, practically waving its branches, nearly shouting their name. It really seems to hit people like an epiphany. In fact, in some cases the trees themselves have inspired the whole project. *That tree needs a treehouse*, people say to themselves. That's more or less what happened at the old Gibbs ranch in Montana, site of one of the treehouses described in this book (see Chapter 5). So, even if you've got hundreds of trees to choose from, a leisurely stroll on the property will probably reveal the right one—the "chosen" tree. Before you set out exploring the woods, think of it this way: your treehouse is already there. All you have to do is see it—then put some wood around it.

## Finding a Healthy Tree

**S**o you've found it. It's the right height, it's facing the right way, it's in the right location. But . . . is it healthy? Is it a good treehouse species? These may be the most important questions of all. Some trees make for great hosts, others mediocre. In general, you want to go with mature, hard-to-medium woods. The stronger the tree the better. And the more mature it is, the less it will grow and cause your treehouse to shift. I can't stress how important it is to do tree research. Here are some basics to keep in mind when giving a tree a "checkup."

## Roots

Just as the tree is the foundation of your treehouse, the roots are the foundation of any tree. Inspect your tree's roots thoroughly for any sign of trouble. Check out the root crown (where the roots flare out into the soil at the base of the trunk) for disease. In most trees, a healthy root crown should look like a trumpet set upright on a table, resting on its flared bell. If the crown has been buried by regrading, the buttress tree roots could actually suffocate. Building in a tree in this state is a potential hazard, but it's not always easy to spot this sort of trouble.

If for some reason the root crown isn't showing, you should check for evidence of regrading. Have you or anyone else been building in the area, or moving dirt around? Are there signs of landscaping or construction near the tree? If you suspect the roots have been buried a bit, expose them down to about a foot below the normal root crown flair. Scuff the roots very lightly with a chisel to see beneath the bark. A healthy root should be bright pink to red, or green. If you find disease or decay in more than half of a root's circumference, the tree is probably in bad shape and shouldn't even be climbed.

If your root crown is particularly shallow, as it is with beech trees, for example, look around to see if there are signs of abuse. Do cars travel regularly over the root area, possibly causing damage? Many trees are sensitive to soil compaction; it's particularly tough on oaks and beeches.

Many large shade trees can have a healthy-looking canopy even if the tree has been weakened by root loss or a "girdling" injury, where roots from competing vegetation wrap around the main roots of the tree and cut off their circulation. Some trees send out adventitious, or auxiliary, roots to compensate for damaged anchoring roots. The new roots can keep the tree green but might not be strong enough to keep it upright for very long, especially if you add on the additional weight and wind load of a treehouse.

## Pests and Disease

If the roots check out, it's time to look skyward. First check the leaves or needles to see if they're in good condition. If they're dry and crumbly (and it's not autumn),

Right Tree, Wrong Tree

there could be something wrong. Look up to the canopy. What's happening up there? Is it dried out and gray? Have all the top leaves fallen off? These are signs of problems.

Check for insect infestations. A tree full of wood-eating bugs is a tree to avoid at all costs. You'll also want to inspect neighboring trees to see if they're infested as well. Find out what tree diseases and destructive pests are common in your area. Up in Alaska, Gus Gunther was very worried about BeetleKill, a disease caused by beetles. Some on the east coast of the United States may remember Dutch elm disease from two decades ago, or the Gypsy moths that periodically ravage trees in New England and the north Atlantic states. Most critters that infest trees advertise themselves in one way or another. Find a book on tree ailments at a local library or nursery and use it as a reference tool. And get to know the arborists, or tree experts, at that nursery—their help will keep you, your treehouse, and your tree going for much longer.

## Tree Maintenance

Once your tree has passed its physical, you'll want to *keep* it healthy. People are always talking about preventive medicine, or "wellness." The same approach to health works with trees. There are a few basic things you can do to keep your tree healthy.

## Clearing and Thinning

Clear debris and vegetation away from the root system. This keeps the roots breathing and free from competition for nutrients and water. Grass is a particularly savage sapper of strength. Clear an area as wide as the circumference of the branches above it. To make sure the soil isn't overly depleted by clearing, spread mulched compost or woodchips (use chips of conifers if it's a conifer, or from deciduous trees if it's deciduous) around the tree. It's also a good idea to feed the tree with tree fertilizer. When and how much should be explained on the fertilizer packaging. If not, an arborist can advise you on your particular tree.

Remove any dead wood and snags from among the branches of the tree. This relieves the tree of extra weight and helps prevent the spread of disease (dead branches often have died from infections). Snags also pose the threat of falling onto your treehouse roof—or on you.

## Pruning

Pruning is essential. I look at it this way: Your treehouse is going to weigh a lot, so it will be a relief to the tree to have some branches thinned out. Pruning also increases light penetration and air movement, and decreases wind resistance. And if you prune properly, you'll enhance your views.

I recommend doing all your pruning before you build your treehouse. Most of what I learned about pruning I learned *after* I'd finished my treehouse office. It's going to be much harder to go back and trim branches now that the roof is on. I may still do it one of these days—probably after a branch lands on my head. Sometimes that's the only wake-up call I answer to. Oh well. I would also strongly recommend you contact a local arborist if the work is at all intimidating. Pruning is a job that can get pretty hairy, particularly in a large tree, and you don't want to psych yourself out before you even get started. You also don't want to damage the tree by pruning too much; the arborist can help with that.

You can trim smaller branches easily with a hand or electric saw, but with bigger branches you need to prepare a bit more. One good rule: If you can't support the weight of the branch with your arms, tie a line to it first. As you cut, keep the line taut, so when the branch comes loose it won't free-fall onto something or someone. Lower it carefully to the ground.

For aesthetic reasons it is good to trim branches just beyond the collar where it joins the trunk or parent branch. Don't use wound dressing to seal or protect cuts. Experts say there's no proof the dressing actually improves the tree's health; it may even make the tree more susceptible to disease by trapping moisture against the wound and cutting off air circulation.

If you've chosen a tree in a thick forest, you may want to prune neighboring

Arborist Jonathan Fairoaks performs his magic high in the branches of Doug Thron's giant madrona tree in Northern California. The larger branches of this single tree will be cabled together above the roofline of the future treehouse.

Right Tree, Wrong Tree

trees to increase sunlight and improve your view, or remove close trees altogether to reduce competition and the potential for the spreading of disease.

## Other Tips

If you're building in one tree with multiple trunks, and your treehouse is placing strain on them, it's prudent to tie the trunks together with cable above your treehouse. Again, an arborist is trained in exactly this sort of work and can help you make sure all the trunks have adequate support.

If you build a particularly large treehouse, you might create a rain block that keeps water from reaching the roots of the tree. A soaker hose used occasionally below the tree would be a good idea. But be careful not to irrigate tree trunks directly; experienced arborists have noticed serious disease and structural problems resulting from sprinkler irrigation hitting a tree's trunk.

## Types of Trees

So which trees are the best to build in? This is one of the obvious questions a future treehouse builder will ask. The answer is, you can build a treehouse in any species of tree, but some are more suitable than others. The list below gives a general assessment of the trees I'm familiar with, but there are dozens of others that I still haven't worked in.

### TREE CHARACTERISTICS

| Best | Characteristics |
| --- | --- |
| **Apple** | Classic for kids' treehouses. Easy, low access. Strong. Full of yummy apples for eating and throwing. |
| **Ash** | Beautiful when healthy, but watch out for disease when stressed. Ash blight in northeast U.S. right now. |
| **Banyan** | Grows very fast, and will throw your treehouse out of |

whack quickly, so be prepared. Fun to watch your tree and treehouse intertwine and become one within five years.

**Baobab**      Native to Africa. If you have one, please call me immediately.

**Fir**      A mature fir is a great treehouse tree. Below a certain level there are not many support branches so it is often necessary to incorporate more than one tree (see Fall City office treehouse). Giant firs can even support single tree designs. Long life span.

**Hickory**      Extremely hard wood. Tough wood to bolt to, but very durable.

**Madrona**      Very hard wood. Often has multiple trunks for interesting designs, but tread lightly: It's sensitive to disease. Use cabling to reinforce trunks. Beautiful, common to U.S. and Canadian west coasts.

**Mango**      Durable and strong. Has many low branches for easily accessible treehouses. Good for kids' treehouses.

**Maple**      Durable, fast growing. Requires careful thinning if mature. Size and softer wood can make it susceptible to storm damage. Sugar maple best of all maples for treehouses because of its plentiful support branches and excellent durability.

**Monkey Pod**      Great tree. Perfectly suited for large treehouses. They are strong, durable, and consistently form perfect house sites at 25 feet off the ground. Only in your wildest dreams would you be so lucky to build in one. Native to South America and can be found in Hawaii.

**Oak**        Very durable, but sensitive to soil compaction and grade changes. The white oak is one of the most beautiful giants in the forest and makes an excellent host.

**Palm**       Extremely flexible. Trunk-mount only and through-bolt all connections. Watch out for falling coconuts.

**Pine**       Grows fast, straight. Not many support branches. Moderately durable. Don't pee on it—it's salt-intolerant.

**Spruce**     Medium-dense soft wood, but susceptible to insects. Shallow roots. Go with multiple tree designs for added support.

---

*Marginal*

---

**Alder**      Brittle branches, short life span, prone to infections, grows quickly.

**Black Walnut** Brittle, branches snap easily. Beware.

**Cottonwood** Weak-wooded, messy seed pods. Avoid suspension designs.

**Elm**        Prone to many pests and diseases. Often devastated by Dutch elm disease.

**Sycamore**   Brittle, branches snap easily. Susceptible to insects and disease. Short-lived in urban conditions.

2

# A Treehouse for Small People

**Now that you know a bit more about how to approach a** treehouse project, it's time to get started building. When I first began building treehouses, I decided to start small, by building a house for small people. Walking through a very basic kids' treehouse will help you understand some of the building techniques that you can apply to any size structure but which are easier to execute on a smaller scale. A kids' treehouse will also get you quickly acquainted with my unique approach to treehouse building. It might seem a bit unorthodox at first, but it works. My focus is on building treehouses quickly, cheaply, lightly, safely—with lots of fun and silliness thrown in. After all, we're not building pianos here. We're building ships in the air, right? We're building crow's nests to spot land on the horizon! We're building whatever it is your imagination wants.

SOME OF MY GENERAL RULES FOR BUILDING TREEHOUSES, LARGE AND SMALL, INCLUDE:

• Build as much of the house as possible on the ground. This rule will save you more headaches and frustration than any other. If you can build your platform on the

---

*Photo at top of page:* **Happy homeowners.**

ground, do it. If you can frame and side the walls on the ground, do it. If you can attach doors and windows on the ground, do it. You see what I'm getting at: Anything that you can accomplish with both feet firmly planted on Earth should be done that way; after all, that's where your tools are. When evolution erased our tails, it's where we learned about balance and gravity. Besides, our goal is not to forsake the ground entirely, like young Cosimo in Italo Calvino's *The Baron in the Trees* (see Further Reading, page 169). We're just trying to get away from it for a little while. Because the dimensions on a kids' treehouse are small, you can assemble most of the pieces below the tree, then hoist them up one by one. With adult treehouses, much more of the building happens in the air.

- Keep your dimensions simple. It just makes the math that much easier. In the treehouse you're about to see, the platform is $4 \times 6$ feet. The floor joists (supports nailed to the bottom of the platform) are set at nice, even 2-foot intervals. This makes conceptualizing easier and cuts down dramatically on measurement errors.

- Use power tools if you have them—a table saw is great for ripping (cutting with the grain of the wood) odd-size trim and drip-edge details—but don't sweat it if you don't. A chop saw is great for cross cutting through your studs, joists, and rafters, but with a kids' treehouse, those materials are few enough that a handsaw will suffice. In fact, the main tools you really need for a kids' treehouse are few: a saw, a hammer, a drill, a level, a wrench, and maybe a screwdriver.

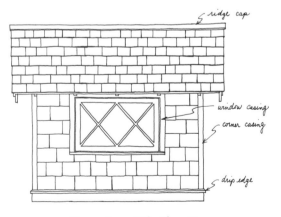

ridge cap

window casing

corner casing

drip edge

**Figure 2 • Side Elevation**

By the way, don't forget that your own kids make the best carpenter's helpers. Getting them involved in the project will give them a sense of ownership. This is so important. More than once I've been involved in a kids' treehouse project where the parents and I designed and constructed the whole beautiful thing, only to discover the children had gone off and built their own with scavenged supplies from our site. A tree-house gives children a sense of safe separation from their moms and dads. If you build the treehouse without consulting them on design or letting them bring you more nails as you run out, they might not feel like it's theirs. Without that sense, they won't hang out there.

Two safe tasks I've had luck with over the years are having the kids wash the treehouse windows on the ground (if you've found them secondhand, they'll be very dirty) and letting them practice pounding nails. To do the latter I drill a bunch of pilot holes in scrap wood. The kids can set the

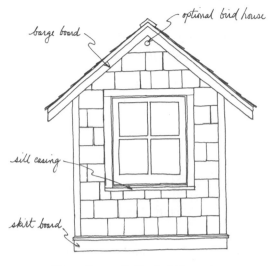

**Figure 3  •  Gable End Elevation**

nails in the holes and bang them in. Sometimes this is more captivating than—dare I say it—the television. And they're learning at the same time: how to sink a nail straight, how much a hammer against a finger hurts, how much satisfaction there is in carpentry. It might even serve as a reminder to you.

Ready to go? So go. As you'll see, this project is modest enough that if you make any mistakes, correcting them will only take a couple of minutes. This treehouse took me two leisurely days to construct. If you're going to build your kids something like this, a lazy weekend should suffice. Any additional detail work can come later.

## Charlie and Henry's Treehouse

### Setting Up Your Work Site

The following is a list of the basic tools you'll need:

>  a level building area

>  a flat work surface or a workbench at least 4 × 8 feet in size. (I set up a worktable made from ½-inch plywood and two-by-fours that measured

*5 × 8 feet on the surface and stood 36 inches off the ground. This was ideal for building all of the components of the house, including the platform.)*

*circular saw*

*hammer*

*level*

*power drill and screwdriver*

*framing square, bevel square, speed square*

*crescent wrench or socket wrench*

*chalk line*

Most children's treehouses use rigid platform designs—that is, they usually do not allow for much flexibility between trees or limbs. We used this style of platform in this house because it's the easiest way to build, but we managed to place it in the tree in a way that would allow the support branches to continue to move and flex independently.

## The Platform

The floor plan of this treehouse is as simple as they get. It is a 4 × 6-foot rectangular box with a trapdoor, set 6 feet above the ground in an apple tree. With such short distances for the wood to span, it is okay to use two-by-fours for the floor framing.

First take a 4 × 8-foot sheet of ⅝-inch CDX plywood and cut 2 feet off of the 8-foot dimension. The plywood should now measure 4 × 6 feet. Now you can see exactly what size structure we are building here. Next, cut your floor joists. These components run under the plywood floor, on edge, and support it. Cut two 2 × 4s at 72 inches, five at 45 inches, and two at 21¾ inches to form a box for the trapdoor. The 72-inch pieces are called the rim joists. They sandwich the 45-inch pieces called the floor joists and create the structural framework for your platform. The 21¾-inch pieces will form a box around an opening for the trapdoor entry we'll cut between the floor joists. With all of the pieces in hand, go to your worktable and place the two rim joists together on edge. Mark them so you will know where to nail the 45-inch joists.

I use 24-inch centers for the joists. In other words, I nail a floor joist every 24

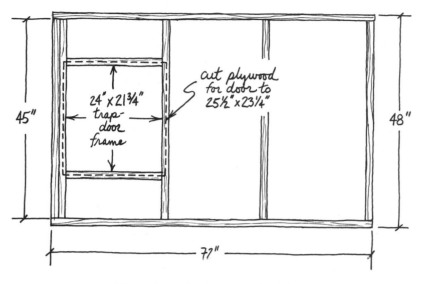

**Figure 4  •  Platform Framing Plan**

inches. This is a wide spacing, but it provides more than enough strength for a child's treehouse. The wide spacing also helps keep the weight to a minimum, which is also a big consideration in treehouse construction. Mark a point every 24 inches along your rim joist. Then pull back ¾ of an inch from that point and draw a line across both rim joists with a square while you squeeze them together on edge. That ¾ inch represents half the width of a joist. These lines will give you a mark to line up the edge of your floor joists with.

Before you nail everything together, decide where to place the entry hatch. Since the design calls for a trapdoor entry, the floor framing has to be arranged in a way to accommodate this, so you'll have to think ahead a few steps. In our example, the shape and direction of the tree branches meant we had to put the trapdoor between a floor joist and one of the end joists to ensure clear access to it from below. However, this created a small problem: The trapdoor hatch can't rest on the end joist, so we added a second joist butted up against the end joist for support (see Figure 4). I marked two of the 45-inch joists to create a box for the trapdoor. I chose to center the door and made it 24 inches wide.

The box is the first part of the floor framing that I put together, nailing the 21¾-inch pieces into the 45-inch floor joists, then nailing the floor joists into the rim

🌳  A Treehouse for Small People

joists. By nailing it together now you can avoid tricky toenailing later (nailing on an angle).

Now line up the remaining floor joists with the marks on the two rim joists and nail away. I put three 16-penny galvanized nails in each connection.

**A 1 x 2 straightedge helps ensure even shingling.**

Don't worry if the framing looks out of square. The plywood solves that. Before I nail on the plywood, however, I like to mark and cut the trapdoor opening. Make this ¾ inch wider on all sides than the opening of the framed box. This will create the lip to rest the door on and keep it from falling open.

Now you can nail the plywood to the frame. Since you are also using this plywood to square the frame, be sure all of the edges line up before you begin to nail. I use 8-penny nails spaced every 6 to 8 inches.

## PUTTING THE PLATFORM IN THE TREE

One of the reasons I chose to frame the platform on the ground was because it would have made me crazy to try to figure out precisely where all of the points of a flat 4 × 6-foot rectangle would hit the multiple limbs of the host apple tree. From my initial observation of the tree, I knew only that it would fit somewhere. As long as I could rest most of the weight on two main parts of the tree, I figured it would be adequately supported by one means or another at other points. (As it turned out, we ended up posting down one corner with a 4 × 4-inch post.) I hoisted the platform into the tree. When we found a spot we were happy with, I marked the points of intersection on the main support limbs and pulled the platform back out of the tree.

## CONNECTING THE TREEHOUSE PLATFORM BACK TO THE TREE

Once the points of intersection are marked on the main support branches of the apple tree, the next order of business is to decide how exactly to secure the platform to the tree. In this example, the apple tree is still relatively young and even the main support branches have some flexibility. It would be possible to simply drill holes through the support branches and send long bolts all the way through, directly into the platform framing. To give it a little more flexibility, however, I chose to fix two points in the manner I just described and then create a "floating" point load at the two other points where the platform intersected the tree. One corner of the platform was still left unsupported despite my best efforts to position the platform in a way that it could be supported entirely by the tree. Here I simply posted down to the ground with a 4 × 4. I know it sounds like cheating, but I also know the tree appreciates it and I think that's really all that counts.

To begin the process of installing the platform, I created the two floating points first. Here I built a kind of heavy-duty shelf that was fabricated out of a short piece of pressure-treated 4 × 8. At the point of intersection marked on the branch I held up the short section of 4 × 8 as level as possible and with a pencil marked a line that closely approximated the angle of the branch upon which the "shelf" would rest. After a few passes with the skill saw I was satisfied with a wedge-shape piece of wood that I could then bolt directly to the support branch. For safety I added a strong metal clip at the end of the shelf to prevent the platform from ever slipping off. I repeated the same process on the other floating point.

With the floating points installed I was then able to place the platform back into the tree. The floating points supported one end of the platform and now it was time to level across the 6-foot length of the platform and set some temporary support posts so that the other connections could be made. Once leveled, the platform was easily supported with two 2 × 2s at the corners opposite the floating points.

Just to be sure everything checked out, I put the level back up on the platform and checked both directions. Now is the time to make any adjustments.

For the two fixed points I drilled holes directly through the support branches and into the rim joists of the platform. Rather than pull the platform tight against the limb, however, I used a short section of galvanized pipe as a spacer. This spacer

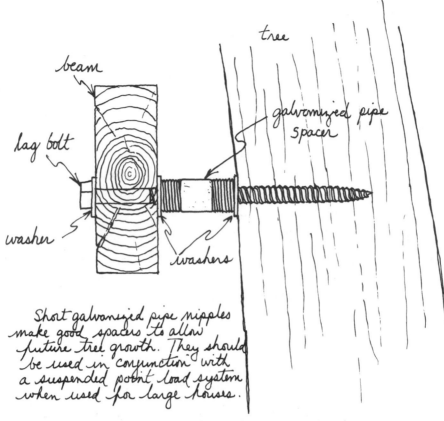

beam

lag bolt

washer

tree

galvanized pipe spacer

washers

Short galvanized pipe nipples make good spacers to allow future tree growth. They should be used in conjunction with a suspended point load system when used for large houses.

**Figure 5 • Galvanized Pipe Spacer Detail**

might be 2 inches or so long, and fits like a sleeve over the galvanized bolt. I used a washer on both sides of the spacer (and a third at the head of the bolt) so that the pipe wouldn't dig into the tree when the bolt was tightened. This spacer serves as a relief valve so the tree can continue to grow and not be restricted by the entire face of a 2 × 4. (Later I will discuss ways of attaching larger structures to trees.) This method of attachment works well for relatively light children's treehouses, but a spacer for a heavier treehouse should be incorporated into a suspended attachment system, which I will discuss on page 51. Otherwise the face on the bolt can be too great and could potentially shear the bolt off or bend it dramatically.

The final point of attachment was made by bolting a 4 × 4 post to the inside corner of the platform using two ½ × 5½-inch galvanized carriage bolts. Checking the platform level one more time, measure down to a precast concrete post anchor that you can bury in the ground. In our case we ran into a major root where the concrete pier was to be placed, so we used a section of pressure-treated 2 × 8 and buried it flush with the ground on its side to provide a base for the post. Cut your 4 × 4 post and set it into position. I like to put a nail or two in it to hold it in position before I break out the drill and bore the holes for the carriage bolts. At the bottom I toe-nailed with screws into the pressure-treated wood base once I had the post leveled in both directions. Now your platform is complete. Climb on up and give it the test. If it holds, move on. There's still a lot of work to be done!

## Building the Walls

I use a lightweight panelized wall system that is simple to build and, once in place, screws together with 3-inch self-tapping wood screws.

This treehouse is made of four separate wall panels and two roof panels. The wall panels include two end panels that are each alike and have the gable end built into them. (The gable is the triangular shape created by two roof planes that meet at a peak.) The two remaining rectangular side wall panels are alike as well. The roof panels are identical and span the 6-foot length of the treehouse on both sides of the gable. These too are rectangular.

Before we get into the details of how to build these panels, let me explain the basics of how the system works. To borrow some terms from conventional wood-frame construction, the walls of your treehouse are made up of two particular types: by-walls and butt-walls. Visualize this treehouse as a 4 × 6-foot rectangular box with four sides. The simplest way to build that box is to sandwich two equal-length opposite walls between the other two equal-length walls. The sides being sandwiched will "butt" into the sides doing the sandwiching; the sides doing the sandwiching run "by" the sides they sandwich. With our treehouse, the two 4-foot-wide gable-end walls run "by" the side walls. The two side walls "butt" into the gable-end walls.

Why is that important? In building treehouses you want to do as much of the work safely on the ground as possible. This includes building your walls and installing siding, windows, window casing (the wood trim around the windows), doors, door casing, shingles, and corner trim. For everything to fit together properly within your overall dimensions when it is all raised up into the tree, you must keep in mind which walls are the "by-walls" and which are the "butt-walls." For example, the by-walls will have the corner trim attached. The butt-walls need no corner trim, but will need to be shortened in length by the depth, or thickness, of the by-walls that they butt into at both ends, to maintain the specified length of that side of the house (6 feet in this case, which means the butt-walls will have to be shortened 3 inches to make room for the by-walls at both ends). With this in mind now we can start building our walls.

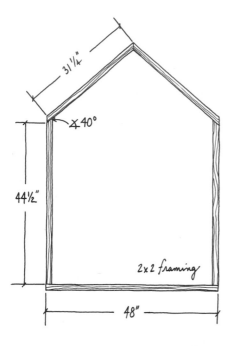

**Figure 6 • Perimeter Framing Plan—
Gable End**

## FRAMING

In the interest of keeping this little treehouse as light as possible, I'd use a combination of 1 × 2 and 2 × 2-inch framing. As we get into larger structures later in the book, you will see how framing a treehouse can change, but when building small, this framing method works best.

First, let's build a perimeter frame of 2 × 2s. Before you begin assembling it, however, do a life-size drawing of the outside edge of the frame. Do this directly on your worktable or, if your platform is still on the ground, draw it on that. This is called a full-scale layout and is very helpful for visualizing and taking measurements for the framing.

Start with the gable end. Since this is a by-wall, it will run the full 4 feet along its base. Mark this length on the edge of your table. The height of this design runs 4 feet tall. Measure up 4 feet at right angles from the ends of your first measurement and mark those points on your layout. Now it is time to figure out the slope of your roof, or the triangular section that connects with the roof panels.

The roof pitch (as the slope is called in carpenters' terms) is determined by measuring by how much the roof rises versus how long it runs. Common roof pitches range from a low slope of 3-in-12 pitch (a roof that rises 3 feet over 12 feet) to a relatively steep slope of 12-in-12 pitch. A 12-in-12 pitch would form a 45-degree angle at the corner with the wall. Rather than go with a simple 12-in-12 for this design, I decided to make things more challenging and use a 10-in-12 pitch for this roof; I think it looks better than the steeper pitch. (There *are* certain things that I'm finicky about in treehouse design.)

To transfer a roof line to your full-scale layout at the proper pitch, measure up 20 inches from the two marks at 48 inches. Now mark a straight line that connects these two points. I highly recommend using a chalk line, but if you don't have one, a good straightedge will do. Measure out on that new line 24 inches and put a mark there. Connect that point with the two points at 48 inches with a straight line. There you have the outline of your wall frame.

Here it is again in slow motion: Since we chose a 10-in-12-pitch roof, for every 12 inches of horizontal run, the roof rises 10 inches. The peak is at the center of the 4-foot wall, so we know the run will be at 2 feet, or 24 inches. To stick with the 10-in-12 pitch, the roof will need to rise 20 inches. This is why we added 20 inches to the wall line.

Now you have a life-size model from which you can take measurements. The first piece I cut is the bottom piece, called the bottom plate. (Later on in the book we will describe in detail all of the components of a frame wall, but for now I will only introduce you to a few.) Cut your bottom plate to 48 inches out of a 2 × 2. After that, cut your roof peak pieces (top plates) from the same material. To do this, use a bevel square and place it on the layout to find the proper roof angle. We know that angle is 40 degrees since it is a relatively common roof pitch. With your bevel

**The gable end wall is complete.**

🌳 A Treehouse for Small People

square transfer that angle to one end of a length of 2 × 2. If you are lucky enough to have a chop saw, set the angle to 40 degrees. To find the length of your cut, measure the full-scale layout from the 48-inch wall mark to the center peak. Transfer that to your 2 × 2 and make the cut. You will need two of these pieces, so make that same piece again.

To come up with the proper size for the vertical wall pieces (corner studs), set the bottom plate and the two top plates in their positions on the layout. Now trace the inside edge of these pieces directly onto your work surface. The distance between these lines is the length of your corner studs. The tops will have the same angle as your roof plates, so that the roof plates sit flush on the wall frame.

Nail all of this together directly on top of your full-scale layout. I like to nail this perimeter frame down to my work surface with small finish nails just to be sure it holds its shape while I move to the next phase—filling in the remaining studs.


### SIDING CONSIDERATIONS

You have to decide what, if any, type of siding to use. I have always been fond of cedar shingles, so I used them here. Choosing your siding now is important because your framing method depends on it. We will have more to say about this later in the book, but for now let's stick with the immediate issue: Using shingles means you need something to nail them to. That something is called sheathing. Often it's plywood. Since kids' treehouses usually don't have finished interiors, and because cedar shingles look almost as good from the back as they do from the front, I opted out of plywood sheathing and went with 1 × 2-inch skip sheathing, which is basically strips of wood that run horizontally across the framing at set intervals. It provides a backing to nail my shingles on without the weight of plywood.

To accommodate the sheathing, I decided to make the remaining (inside) studs 1 × 2s, not the 2 × 2s that we used for the perimeter frame. Since 1 × 2s are actually 1½ inches wide by ¾ inch deep, you can set these studs flush against the *inside* edges of the perimeter frame and still have a space of ¾ inch on the outer edge—just enough room for the skip sheathing. When the 1 × 2-inch sheathing is set against the inside studs, it makes up that difference in space and lines up flush with the outside of the 2 × 2-inch perimeter frame. This makes for a nice, neat package that is also quite strong.

## MAKING ROOM FOR WINDOWS

Before you fill in the walls with the 1 × 2s, keep in mind that you are building a treehouse and that a treehouse should have lots of windows, with or without glass. I am always on the lookout for old windows that people are throwing away, so out of my collection I pulled two identical four-pane windows for the house's front and back. These measured 24 × 29 inches each.

Windows don't sit directly against the studs of a wall. They have their own frame, or jamb, that itself attaches to the wall. The only thing you need to consider before building the window jambs is their thickness. I build children's window jambs from 1× (that is, ¾-inch thick) cedar stock cut down to a width of 1½ inches. That means each side of the jamb is ¾ inch thick. The window itself is 24 inches wide, so the total width of the window and its jamb is 25½ inches. Just to make sure the window fits, let's leave an additional ⅛ inch on both sides between the window and the jamb. So now our final width is 25¾ inches. You must accommodate this space as you're laying out your inside studs.

Make your stud marks directly on the perimeter frame that you have nailed to the work surface. On the bottom plate find the center at 24 inches and mark it. This will be the line from which to center your window. Take half of the 24-inch width of the window, add the ¾ inch for the jamb and ⅛ inch for play, and pull that distance (12⅞ inches) off both sides of the center line mark and mark that. Come back and use your square to extend those marks across

**Attaching the hinges on the ground makes windows easier to install.**

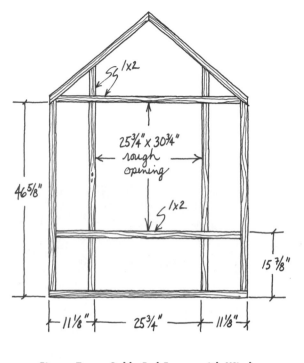

25¾" x 30¾" rough opening

1x2

1x2

46⅝"

15⅞"

11⅛"    25¾"    11⅛"

**Figure 7  •  Gable End Frame with Window
Rough-Framed**

the full width of the bottom plate. (I like to put an "X" on the side of the line that the new stud will lie on.)

Marking the stud mark on the top plate of the full-scale layout is a bit trickier. You'll need a framing square and a straight 6-foot-long 1 × 2. Lay the 1 × 2 across the frame beginning at one of your stud marks on the bottom plate. Then use the framing square to make sure the 1 × 2 runs at a right angle off the bottom plate. Make a mark to one side of the 1 × 2 where it passes over the sloping roof plate. The bottom of the stud will have a straight cut but the top will have the same 40-degree angle that the top plate and the corner studs have. Cut two pieces, one for each side of the window. Nail these pieces in place with 12-penny finish nails (16-penny framing nails are a bit thick and may cause some splitting problems).

Next, you need to decide at what level you want to start the window. I chose to match the sill heights of the windows on the gable end walls with those on the side walls.

I set the sill height for the rough opening at 15⅞ inches. The head height, therefore, was arrived at by adding the height of the window (29 inches), the thickness of the jamb (¾ inch at top and bottom), and ¼ inch for play. That amount plus the 15⅞-inch sill height totals 46⅝ inches from the base of the wall. Mark both studs with the sill and head measurements and put an "X" on the side of the mark where this horizontal framing will lie. Measure and cut these pieces from a 1 × 2. Here is how to do it: Cut the 1 × 2, place it into the frame, and nail it through the perimeter 2 × 2 with 12-penny finishing nails to secure the ends. Use two 1½-inch nails per connection where the sill piece crosses the studs. The header piece will need angles cut on its ends to fit within the perimeter frame. As you can see in Figure 7, the bottom half of the header is 45 inches long, just like the sill. The top half has a 50-degree angled cut to accommodate the roof plates.

Congratulations! Now you have the framing for the window in the center of your emerging wall. This is called the rough opening for your window and should measure 25¾ inches wide by 30¾ inches tall. You have tackled all of the difficult cuts and angles, and now you are well on your way to understanding the basics of treehouse framing!

### INSTALLING THE SKIP SHEATHING

Now it's time to fill in the frame with the horizontal skip sheathing. This procedure begs a question: What kind of exposure do you want for the shingles? That is, how much of the shingle do you want to see? I usually plan on 6 inches. So, since the shingles will overlap each other every 6 inches, you should lay out the sheathing every 6 inches measuring from the bottom edge. This puts the skip sheathing right where we'll nail the shingles on. A 1 × 2 does not give a very wide nailing surface (1½ inches), so it is important to place the skip sheathing accurately. I start by marking all the way up the inside edges of the corner wall studs every 6 inches starting from the base. These marks indicate the bottom edge of each row of shingles and also mark the bottom edge of the 1 × 2-inch skip sheathing.

On the gable end wall you'll have only two sheathing pieces that run the full 45-inch length of the frame below the

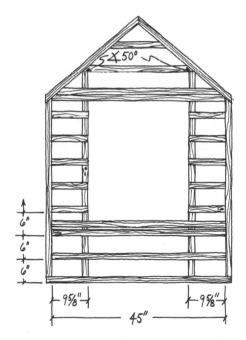

**Figure 8 • Gable End Frame with 1 x 2 Skip Sheathing**

window. Along the sides of the window, you must cut short pieces of skip sheathing that will run from the perimeter frame flush to the inside of studs at the rough opening. Transfer your 6-inch marks to the face of your studs to maintain a consistent spacing of the sheathing.

When you reach the slope of the roof, use the same 50-degree angle you used for the window header piece. Mark your 6-inch increments on the slope pieces by pulling your tape all the way from the bottom plate. Be careful to keep your tape measure parallel to the studs when marking the points. Like the other skip sheathing markings, these also represent the bottom edge. Measure from one mark across to the corresponding mark on the other roof plate. Cut a 50-degree angle; it should fit. Nail the sheathing in. When you have finished, the wall is ready to be trimmed and sided. We'll get to the side wall sheathing in a minute, but, first, we need to frame it!

### FRAMING THE SIDE WALLS

Before jumping into the siding phase, I like to finish framing all of the walls. If you are lucky enough to have some helpers, the siding can happen while the framing continues. Let me explain how I framed the remaining walls on this house.

One of the advantages of building a simple treehouse like this is that the gable end walls are exactly alike and the side walls are exactly alike. Since you know from your full-scale layout how to build the gable end and the marks are still clear on the work surface, I suggest you go ahead and build this same wall while it is still fresh in your mind. In fact, if you are really on top of the situation, you may have seen this coming and already cut two pieces for each piece I described. That would qualify you instantly for the Star Student Award.

There are no complicated angles to deal with on this side wall frame. All you need to do first is figure out where to set the window and how long to cut the pieces.

Again, start with cutting the plates or perimeter pieces. In this case you are building a straight wall without a peak. The top plate is therefore the same length as the bottom plate. Since the side wall is acting as the butt-wall, we also know that 1½ inches need to be cut from both ends to allow for the gable end by-walls. Cut your top and bottom plates, therefore, from 2 × 2s at 69 inches.

The height of the side wall is 4 feet. Cut your two perimeter studs at 45 inches (48 inches minus 3 inches from the top and bottom plates). Sandwich your 45-inch studs at the ends of the top and bottom plates and nail away.

Most likely you have something resembling a less-than-square parallelogram. To correct this and make it a perfect rectangle, run your tape measure from opposite corners and adjust the frame until those distances are the same. I call this the "X" check. Once the frame is square, send some finish nails through the frame into your work surface at three points so it doesn't move.

Out of my window stash I picked two identical diamond-patterned windows that measured 36 inches wide by 23 inches tall. You'll already know the beginning height of your windows, since you'll be matching them with the windows on the gable end walls. The only thing you have to decide is how far to the left or right to place them. I decided to center them.

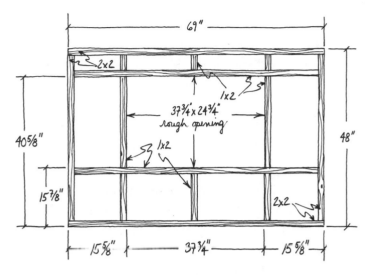

**Figure 9  •  Side Wall Frame with Window Rough-Framed**

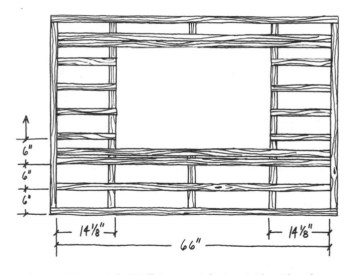

**Figure 10  •  Side Wall Frame with 1 x 2 Skip Sheathing**

Mark the plates as you did on the gable end wall. First, find the center point on the bottom plate (34½ inches) and mark that. Now take half the width of the window (18 inches), plus ¾ inch for the window jamb and ⅛ inch play and mark that distance on both sides of your center point. These points mark the inside edges of the 1 × 2-inch wall studs. Mark your top plate at the same points, then measure, cut, and install your studs. Be careful with that center stud, however, as the window interrupts it. The bottom segment of that stud is 15⅞ inches; the top segment is 5⅞ inches.

To attach the 1 × 2-inch sill piece, mark a point at 15⅞ inches on all the studs. That is the top edge of the sill. Cut your sill to 66 inches. Fit it into position and nail it to the 1 × 2-inch studs and to the end studs. Since the side wall window is 23 inches tall, mark up from the sill piece 23 inches plus the thickness of the window jamb (1½ inches) and ¼ inch for play. From the bottom of the wall, that total length is 40⅝ inches. Mark this height on all your studs, then cut and nail them in. The header, like the sill, is 66 inches long and spans the entire frame. You should now have a wall with a rough window opening of 37¾ × 24¾ inches.

Time to start the side wall skip sheathing. Again, when the skip sheathing is all up, only two 1 × 2s will span the entire length of the wall below the window. Cut those to 66 inches. The rest are 14⅛ inches. Mark 6-inch increments on all your studs, then nail the skip sheathing on. Repeat these exact steps for the identical wall on the opposite side of the treehouse. Take a picture. You've framed your first house.

## Framing the Roof

Since you've just been cutting 1 × 2s, move straight on to framing the roof panels, which are made from the same material. The roof panels are simple to build. The two panels form a gable-style roof—that is, a roof with two sloping planes supported at each end by the triangular extensions of the side walls.

First, you need to decide how much you want the roof to overhang the gable end walls. For a treehouse of this size, I thought 9 inches would look best. As you design and measure the roof frame, you need to make sure to account for the depth of the peak trim you'll nail to the ends once everything's in place. In carpenter parlance, peak trim is called "barge boards." For a more finished look, I usually build a two-piece barge board detail from 1× (¾-inch thick) cedar. The barge board is attached to the outermost rafter, called—wouldn't ya know it—the barge rafter. That adds an extra 1½ inches to the length of the total roof, so your actual roof frame only extends 7½ inches on each side.

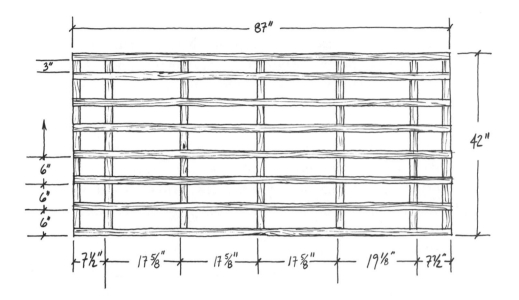

**Figure 11 • Roof Framing Plan**

Rafters are the main structural elements that run perpendicular to the top ridge of the roof and rest on the tops of the walls. The roof sheathing is nailed to the rafters and cedar shingles are nailed to the roof sheathing. It works in much the same way as the wall panels.

The entire roof frame is made with 1 × 2s. I use the same 6-inch shingle exposure as on the walls, so my skip sheathing also runs at 6-inch intervals. Before any cutting begins, however, let's figure out the length and number of roof rafters we'll need. I decided to have a 9-inch overhang over the side walls; to maintain that overhang, the rafters must run 42 inches. Spacing between rafters can be as far apart as 24 inches, but to maintain symmetry and add a bit more strength I set them at 18-inch intervals. That means you'll need seven rafters per roof panel, including the barge rafters on either end. Cut them.

Now let's get the skip sheathing taken care of. We know we have to subtract the 1½-inch width of the barge board on both sides from our overall length. The length is 87 inches. Working on 6-inch intervals, we'll need eight pieces of skip sheathing for each roof frame. Go ahead and cut these as well.

We're ready to assemble. Lay the top and bottom pieces of 87-inch skip

A Treehouse for Small People

sheathing flat on your work surface. On one piece measure in 7½ inches and mark it. (Make all these marks on the short edge of the sheathing.) Put an X on the inside of the mark to indicate that the rafter will rest on that side of your mark. Make the same mark on the other end of the piece. Next, find the center point of the 1 × 2 and mark ¾ inch to one side. Split the distance between the center of the sheathing and the marks at 7½ inches. Mark those points, again pulling off ¾ inch, and you've got yourself all the settings for your rafters. Transfer them all to your other 87-inch piece.

Lay the entire roof panel out on your work surface, with the rafters beneath the two pieces of skip sheathing, all on their respective marks and flush with the ends of the skip sheathing at either end. Start by nailing the two barge rafters to the sheathing with one 1½-inch nail.

As with the side wall, you may now be looking at a less-than-squared frame. You can check the squareness of the roof panels using the "X-check" method. Once it's squared, temporarily nail it to your work surface to hold it in place while you nail on the remaining rafters and skip sheathing. Remember, the skip sheathing runs at 6-inch intervals, measured from one bottom edge to the next. So the actual space between the skip sheathing is 4½ inches. Sink two nails into each connection between the rafters and the sheathing. This helps stabilize the panels and keep them from shifting once you remove the assembly from the work surface.

All right—your roof panel is now done. Follow the same procedure for the other one and we're ready to move on to some more fun stuff.

## Trimming and Siding

The following section shows you how to frame window jambs, build window casings, apply corner trim, and install the shingle siding. Let's start by turning back to the gable end walls and installing the windows.

### INSTALLING WINDOW JAMBS

I usually begin the trimming phase by casing the windows. Casing a window means putting wood trim around its outside edges. But before the casing, you need to build a jamb, or frame, to which the casing is attached.

Building a window jamb is easy. The dimensions of the gable end window are 24 inches wide by 29 inches tall. Cut two pieces of 1× cedar at 29⅛ inches and two at 25⅝. The pieces should be ripped (cut lengthwise) from the 1× cedar to a width of 1½ inches.

You'll notice I suggest cutting the lengths ⅛ inch longer than the window dimensions to make room for the window to open and close without hindrance. If you were planning on nonopening windows, the extra ⅛ inch is unnecessary.

**Screwing in a wall panel to platform.**

Sandwich the 29⅛-inch pieces between the shorter pieces and nail them so the corners are all flush. I recommend gluing these connections first and then nailing them with two 8-penny finish nails. Build a second jamb of this size while you're at it for the other gable end wall. And why not build the side wall window jambs as well—heck, you're on a roll!

Now install the jambs. Place the jamb in the rough window opening flush with the skip sheathing. There should be a little play here but not much. Hold a framing square or speed square at one of the corners to be sure you have a nice square jamb. Secure the jamb by first nailing the bottom into the sill, centered, with 8-penny galvanized finish nails.

At the top of the jamb shim the sides of the frame with cedar shims until the corners are square and flush with the sheathing. Shims are thin wedges of wood used to fill gaps between the jamb and the frame so that when you nail the jamb to the frame, it doesn't get warped or pulled over by the force of the nail being driven into it. The shims may or may not be necessary, depending on how much space there is between the jamb and the frame. Nail the jamb through the shims into the framing.

## Casing the Windows

The casing that wraps around the window attaches to the jamb and skip sheathing. It is common to leave a small piece of the jamb exposed, called a "reveal," when setting a window (or door) casing. I made that reveal ¼ inch. In other words, I hold the

casing back ¼ inch from the inside edge of the window jamb on all four sides. It makes life a little easier if you can use a combination square and a sharp pencil to mark the reveal directly on the jamb. If you don't have a combination square, just use a tape measure and a straightedge.

Start the window casing by cutting the sill, or bottom piece. I cut the sill from 2 × 4-inch cedar by ripping a piece in half on the table saw. Then I run it through the table saw again, putting a 12-degree bevel on the top surface. That helps shed rain away from the wall.

Before I can cut the sill the proper length, I need to decide how wide to make the side pieces of the casing. That's because I want the sill to be flush with their outside edges. I settled on 2¼-inch-wide 1× cedar. Anything wider on such a small building might look clunky. I go ahead and rip two 2¼-inch-wide strips from 1 × 8-inch cedar and hold the pieces up to the casing lines, or reveal, that I've already marked on the jamb. I pull my tape across and measure from the outside edges of the casing. It should read 29⅛ inches. That's the length of my bottom casing. I nail it through the skip sheathing and into the studs using 12-penny galvanized casing nails.

Next, cut the side casing. Using the 2¼-inch-wide strips ripped from stock 1 × 8-inch cedar boards, measure up from the top of the newly installed sill to

**Once bottom plates are screwed down, screw walls to each other at their ends.**

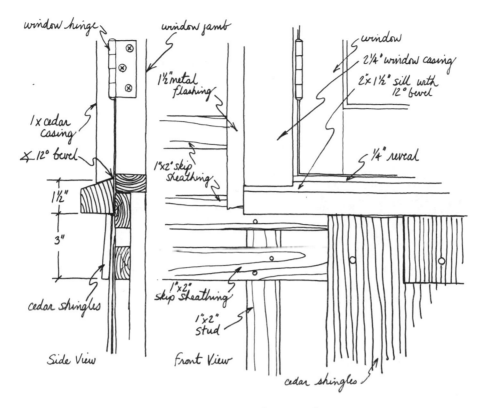

**Figure 12 • Window Details**

the top casing line on the jamb. Mark that distance on your casing board but, instead of making a flush cut, adjust the table on your skill saw to cut a 12-degree angle on the bottom edge which butts the sill. This lets the side casing come down and rest against the sill like a glove. It will also make you feel like the skilled finish carpenter you really are!

Before you actually nail the side casing to the jamb you have to install flashing. The purpose of the flashing is to keep out moisture and to seal the connection where the shingling meets the casing, which can expand and contract depending on temperature and humidity. Flashing is usually made from 1½-inch metal strips. Sometimes people use rubber. Sometimes people bag flashing altogether.

I use flashing only behind the outside edges of the side casing—cut long enough to span from the middle of the sheathing at the sill casing to the middle of the sheathing that the header is nailed to. This way, when the kids are inside, the ends of the flashing are buried behind the sheathing so you won't have to worry about the kids playing near exposed metal edges.

I have a local sheet-metal contractor cut the strips for me out of 10-foot sheets of 26-gauge metal. The strips come with dulled side edges, reducing the danger even further of kids cutting themselves. Cut the length you need with tin snips.

Now line up your side casings with the reveal line on your window jamb. Place the flashing so the ends rest over the appropriate sheathing pieces. The flashing should protrude out from under the outside edge of the side casing by ¾ inch or so.

Nail the casing through the flashing into the skip sheathing at the top and bottom of the span using 7-penny galvanized casing nails. These nails will protrude on the inside, so you'll have to cut them off or bend them when the wall is lifted. Finish nailing the casing to the window jamb with three 7-penny casing nails.

Your top casing spans from outside edge to outside edge of the side casing. Cut that from your 2¼-inch cedar strips and nail it home, right into the sheathing behind it.

**Connect wall panels with 3-inch self-tapping wood screws.**

### TRIMMING THE CORNERS

Since the gable end wall is a by-wall, it will carry the corner trim. This way, when the walls come together there'll be nothing left to do on the exterior but admire a job well done.

Installing the corner trim is easy. The trim covers the two exposed sides of the corner studs. Those sides are 1½ inches wide.

I like both sides of the trim to be the same width. This gets tricky because the trim on the side-wall face of the corner stud butts into the trim on the face of the gable end wall. In other words, in trim runs by the side-wall trim, the thickness of that overlapping piece— ¾ inch—adds extra width to the trim on the side-wall side. Are you still with me? A look at Figure 13 should help.

Cut a 1½-inch-wide strip of 1× cedar and nail it directly to the side-wall face of the corner stud, flush with

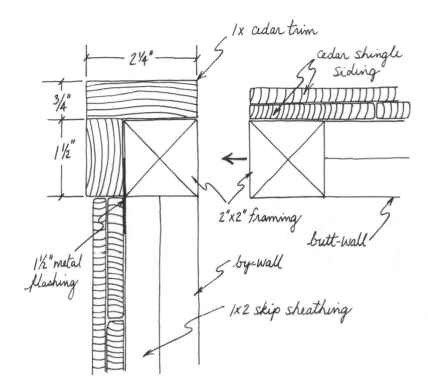

**Figure 13 • Corner Detail Cross Section**

the edge. To the face of the gable end wall nail a strip of 2¼-inch-wide cedar, flush with the end of the trim you just installed. Both pieces of trim run from the base of the wall beyond 48 inches. Trim it later. This creates a net width of 2¼ inches on both sides of the corner. Now both sides match in width. Got it?

There are two other details you will need to attend to before this task is complete. First, you have to install flashing as you did on the window casing. This time the flashing runs from the center of the bottom plate to the center of the top plate, or 46½ inches. It straddles the connection between the trim and the shingles on the gable end side. Attach it exactly the same way as before, making sure its ends are hidden behind the top and bottom plates.

You'll also have to cut the top of the corner trim flush with the top of the top plates to accommodate the slope of the roof. Draw the 40-degree angle right on the two trim pieces and cut them with a skill saw.

🌳    A Treehouse for Small People

## INSTALLING SHINGLE SIDING

I love shingling. It's relaxing, and the cedar smells good. It's therapeutic, though it might appear monotonous at first. It's also a giant chunk of finish work, so it's gratifying. We'll start with the gable end walls.

As I mentioned earlier, I use a 6-inch exposure on all shingles. That is, you can see 6 inches of each shingle protruding from the row above. I use No. 1 or No. 2 sidewall cedar shingles and start at the base of the wall with the undercourse, or lowest row. The undercourse should be flush with the bottom edge of the bottom plate. Start at one inside end of the trim and work your way across, tacking the shingles down with either 5-penny siding nails or 1¼-inch staples directly to the bottom plate. I prefer the staples because they are faster and because I have a pneumatic staple gun. Butt the shingles loosely against each other as you tack them down. As you get toward the far end you can pick through your shingle supply to find one with the right width to complete the row. If you can't find one to fit perfectly in the last bit of space, cut one to size.

**With roof panels secured, structure tightens up considerably.**

Nail the next row of shingles directly over this row but staggering them to cover the seams of the undercourse by at least one inch. Nail those 6¾ inches from the base—at the center of the first row of skip sheathing. The next row of shingles will cover the nails by ¾ inch, keeping them from direct exposure to the elements.

Be sure each successive row overlaps the seams between the shingles of the previous row by at least 1 inch. This ensures water won't get behind the shingles and rot out your walls.

Right off the bat you're going to bump into

the window casing as you work your way up the wall. I like to cut these shingles as precisely as possible. The distance from below the windowsill to the base is 15 inches. Since shingles are usually 16 inches, I cut these down. This meant I now had 9 inches for the next row (15 inches minus the 6-inch exposure = 9 inches), from the shingle line to the bottom of the casing. I cut those and stapled

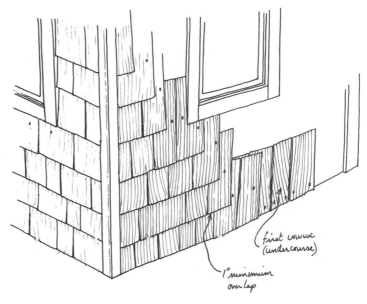

(first course (undercourse)

1" minimum overlap

**Figure 14 • Siding with Cedar Shingles**

them down, also fitting them snugly up against the casing. Measuring from the next shingle line, I had a 3-inch distance. I cut this 3-inch row and attached it with galvanized nails as opposed to staples, which don't have a finished look and rust if left exposed. Notch your shingles appropriately at the windows' edges.

When you get to the sloping top of the wall, stick with your 6-inch exposure and just let the last three rows or so run long and extend over the top edges of the wall. Be sure to nail that top row with the galvanized nails rather than stapling it, since it's exposed and staples would rust. Then go back and mark a line with chalk flush with the top of the

at the top of the wall cut your shingles flush with the top plate at an angle matching the roof pitch

**Figure 15 • Top Row Cut Detail**

wall. Cut the shingles along the chalk line at the same angle as the roof pitch so the roof rafters will rest on the 2 × 2 framing and not the shingles (see figure 15.)

Shingle the other three walls exactly the same way.

  A Treehouse for Small People

## Final Assembly

First, go to your platform and snap chalk lines 1½ inches in from all four edges. Those lines represent the inside edge of the 2 × 2-inch bottom plates of your walls. Line up your walls flush with these lines and they'll also be flush with the outside edge of the platform.

Climb up on the platform and have someone hand you a gable end wall and a side wall. Stand them up more or less on their marks and butt them together, remembering to let the gable end be the by-wall. They should fit together snugly. Now screw the butt-wall stud into the by-wall stud, beginning at the base and working your way up every foot or so. Use 3-inch self-tapping wood screws.

Hoist the remaining two walls onto the platform. Screw the walls together, then screw down through the bottom plates into the platform. Lift the roof pieces into place, making sure the end rafters (not the outermost barge rafters) sit flush on the top plates of the gable end walls. Screw up through the gable end plate into the roof rafters about every foot. Now everything's tightly sealed and . . . wait a minute, you've built yourself into a box! You're trapped! Take it easy—that's what the trapdoor is for. Climb on down and take a gander at your creation.

## Finishing Touches

What's left? Putting in the windows, and the barge boards, finishing the base by adding a drip edge, finishing the trapdoor, and building a ladder.

### The Windows

I usually wait to install windows once the walls are up and the roof is on. In this case, however, since all the components were small and light, I chose to install the windows on the ground. Either way, here is how you do it. The windows on the gable end walls will open out like a door, with hinges on the side. I use 2-inch common hinges, two on each window. To attach the hinges, place them on the appropriate edge on the window and trace them. Chisel those tracings out so the plates sit flush on the window's edge. When that's done screw them to the window. Take the window up in the treehouse and put it in the jamb. Adjust the window to fit evenly in the jamb, then mark the location of the hinges in the edge of the jamb. Now push the window open while holding it so it doesn't fall. When it's wide open there's enough room for you to screw the second hinge plates into the side of the jamb. Line the hinges up with the marks on the jamb and put one screw in each hinge.

Close the window and see how it fits. Make the adjustments, then screw the rest of it in. Attach a simple security bolt to the window and jamb opposite the hinge side to ensure the window stays closed when you want it to. Also, nail a $\frac{1}{2} \times 1$-inch strip of wood across the top of the jamb that sticks down into the window opening by about $\frac{3}{8}$ inch. This will act as a stop and keep the window from opening the wrong way.

The windows on the side walls are awning-style. That is, they're hinged along the top and swing outward and up. Attach the hinges to the windows, and to the top of the jamb—like you did for the gable end windows. I recommend sinking just one screw of each hinge into the jamb, then check to make sure the window swings properly. If it does, then go back and sink the remaining screws.

## THE BARGE BOARDS AND BASE TRIM

The barge boards and base trim add the finishing touches to the outside of your treehouse. These simple details "make" the project.

The barge boards are constructed from 1× cedar. You'll need four $1 \times 4$-inch pieces stretching 3 feet $7\frac{1}{2}$ inches ($43\frac{1}{2}$ inches) from point to point, with parallel 40-degree angles cut on both ends. Now rip four more strips of cedar down to $1 \times 1\frac{1}{2}$ inches, with the same dimensions and angles as the $1 \times 4$s.

I hold both $1 \times 4$-inch strips right up against the barge rafters and press them together at the peak to get a tight fit. Then drop one and nail the other right into the barge rafter. Then nail the other one in, holding it snugly in place. I do the same thing with the $1 \times 1\frac{1}{2}$-inch strips, nailing them flush to the roof shingles and on the $1 \times 4$s I just installed.

The base trim is made up of a ripped $2 \times 2$-inch cedar drip edge that caps a $1 \times 4$-inch cedar "skirt." The skirt and drip edge wrap around all four sides of the treehouse and cover the platform framing. Rip the drip edge from $2 \times 4$-inch cedar to the same profile used for the sill of the window casing. Make four pieces, two roughly 6 feet 6 inches and two roughly 4 feet 6 inches. Cut the pieces to fit along the sides of the treehouse where the walls meet the platform. For the pieces to fit properly, you must "miter" the corners. That means you must cut them at 45-degree angles so they will fit together like a picture frame. Nail these pieces in with 16-penny galvanized casing nails.

The skirt boards are cut to fit just below the drip edge. Since the edges are straight on the skirt boards, you do not need to miter the corners. Cut the pieces so the ends overlap, then nail the pieces directly to the framing below with 7-penny siding nails.

**A table saw is handy for exterior trim and finish work.**

## THE TRAPDOOR

You already cut the trapdoor hole when you were cutting the platform. Now you just need to put the door on it. Grab the square cutout and attach two hinges to it, just as you did with the windows. The hatch should open in. When shut, it rests on the ¾-inch lip left for it when you framed the platform. I drill a hole in the end opposite the hinges that is big enough for a kid's finger to fit through for easy opening.

## WOOD LADDERS

Now the only thing left to do is figure out a way for kids to get up there.

Of course, no kids' treehouse is ever complete without some sort of unorthodox exit and entry mechanism. After all, what kid would take stairs when he can slide, swing, or spin to the ground? Likewise, getting into the tree should be an event.

I think wood ladders make the most sense for kids. They're strong and they're fun. Surprisingly, however, straight wood ladders are hard to find in stores. There are plenty of stepladders to choose from, but no good, old-fashioned, round-rung ladders. So I'll usually build a simple treehouse ladder myself. If you're using a very steep angle, 2 × 4s will work well for the rungs and the stringers (sides). If the slope is more gradual, I recommend 2 × 6s for extra strength. The type of ladder I build is very strong. Between each rung, sistered up against both stringers, are 1 × 4-inch blocks that add extra support.

One note: Do not nail pieces of 2 × 4 into the tree trunk to serve as a ladder. They're dangerous. For one thing, the pieces will eventually spin or pull out as feet pound against them. They also hurt the tree.

There are a lot of other goodies you can build, like fire poles, zip lines, rope ladders, or slides.

When your kids' treehouse is finished, take a walk around the area below the tree to remove any sticks or rocks that a child might fall on. You might even want to add some sand or wood chips under the tree to help cushion a fall. Now take a walk a few feet away and admire your work.

Do you realize what you've done? You've passed the primer course on the basic principles of treehouse construction. You've built a treehouse. Maybe some "kid energy" even rubbed off on you. The next few projects are for adults, and, not surprisingly, much more complex. But before we dive into those, let's take a close look at the most common ways of attaching your treehouse to its host tree.

# 3

## Methods of Attachment

**As I've said, the tree(s) you choose will dictate the way** you build your treehouse, including what kind of foundation you go with. When building a more ambitious treehouse I always recommend getting a final nod from an arborist before starting to build.

There are three main methods of fixing a treehouse to a tree, and usually I choose a combination. These are the *fixed point load*, the *floating* or *sliding point load*, and the *suspended point load*.

### Fixed Point Load

**T**he fixed point load method requires bolting directly into the tree. It allows for no movement and little or no play between the tree and treehouse. It works best if your house is low to the ground, where the strain on the tree is handled by the thick part of the trunk; a fixed foundation at a high altitude will put more strain on the attachment bolts, since a tree tends to sway more the higher up you go. This method is even more stressful if you're using more than one tree—imagine four trees with solid

---

*Photo at top of page:* **Doug Thron's treehouse in California provides a good example of a suspended point load foundation.**

bolts in them, each swaying independently in the wind. Something will give, probably the bolt or the beam it's holding. Fixed attachments work very well if bolting into a single large tree such as a giant fir or redwood.

To avoid damaging the tree, use only one bolt at each attachment point. Two bolts set close together in a vertical line can kill the section of the tree between them. That dead section will eventually rot and give way, allowing the bolt(s) to pull out. Most treehouse point loads can be supported by one properly sized bolt. I like to place the bolt two-thirds of the way down from the top of the beam for added strength.

I also recommend backing up the bolt with a safety cable, set three or four feet higher in the tree. Set tightly, this cable would allow for the use of spacers behind the beam. Spacers are made of short lengths of galvanized pipe (1 to 3 inches) that allow for more comfortable tree growth (see Figure 5). I'll describe the safety cable further in the upcoming section on suspended point loads.

The bigger bolt you use, the better. I typically use ³⁄₄-inch galvanized lag bolts for larger treehouses and try to sink a minimum of six inches into the wood of the tree (not including the bark). Depending on the size of your project, you might want to go with an even thicker bolt, but even in small children's treehouses, I don't go below ¹⁄₂ inch in width.

At some point the size of the beam becomes a more important

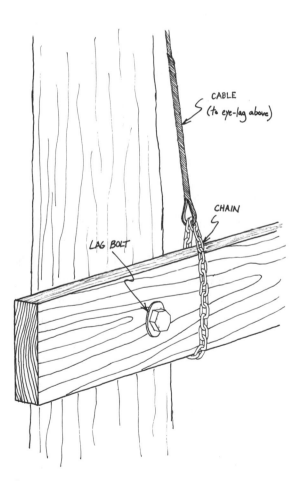

**Figure 16  •  Fixed Point Load with Safety Cable**

Methods of Attachment

factor than the size of the lag bolt. In longer spans of 10 feet or more the danger of a large lag bolt shearing off is less than the danger of your wood beam splitting. I suggest consulting a structural engineer to help size your beams if you plan on building a substantial two-story treehouse. It would also be a good idea to speak with a structural engineer about bolt sizes in general.

Always check the drill curlings from your pilot holes to be sure you are going into firm wood. If you see signs of rot, try a different spot or, if the rot appears pervasive, find a new tree altogether. In any case, never use less than a 6-inch diameter branch for a critical fixed point load.

## Floating Point Load

The floating point load is a good attachment method when using more than one tree or a tree with multiple trunks. Rather than sinking bolts directly into the beams, I attach custom-made channel brackets to the trees for the beams to rest, or "float," on. That way, if the trees move, the beams are free to slide in the brackets. This minimizes the danger of bolt or beam failure, or even tree failure, from the effects of the wind.

I also like to combine the fixed and floating methods when working with more than one tree at moderate heights. At moderate heights the trees, typically, are still relatively straight. Once trunks begin to lean and curve I switch to the suspended method, which I'll describe next. Again, imagine four trees swaying independently in the wind. Four fixed bolts would "trap" the trees, creating all kinds of pressure on both the trees and the platform. So, often I'll fix one end of a beam to one tree, and float the other end on the other tree. If you're worried that the "floating" tree might move so much that the beam could slip right off the bracket, you can add a backup system: an arresting chain that acts as a leash so the end of your beam can't slide all the way off if a tree is really swaying. I always also recommend a safety cable set at least 4 feet higher in the tree.

## Sliding Slot

I have observed a simple homespun method for use in small treehouses that accomplishes the same task as the floating point load without the use of expensive hard-

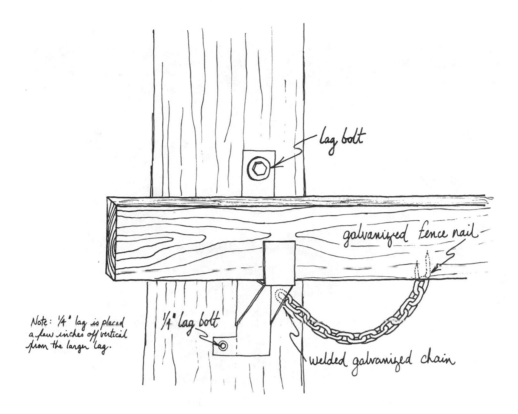

**Figure 17 • Floating or Sliding Point Load with Arresting Chain**

ware. Instead of simply drilling a hole through the beam for your bolt, cut a long slot in the beam ³⁄₁₆-inch wider than the bolt you are using; the length of the slot might be 6 to 8 inches depending on how much play you desire. The beam can now slide along the slot while still being held up by the bolt. Be sure you have a few washers against the tree as well as on the outside of the slot to keep the beam on the bolt.

## Suspended Point Load

**S**uspension connections hang from drop-forged eye-lags screwed into the tree. Common extra-high-strength (EHS) seven-strand cable runs from the lags down to the beams. This cable has a zinc coating bonded directly to the steel and will not peel or flake. You can find it at any specialty hardware store or arborist supply company. In fact, arborists use it regularly to protect homes from trees that are beginning to lean.

**Tree-Grip dead-ends secure a suspended point load foundation.**

The suspension method is the most flexible of the three I use. It works great with any type of tree, especially with trees whose trunks and branches lean in different directions. It's also a great backup for fixed and floating connections. Here's how it works.

The first step is to hoist a beam up to the general area in which you want it to hang, using two ropes, one on either end. Find a place to tie the ropes off, like another tree trunk. With the beam in the tree you'll have a better sense of where and in which branches to set your eye-lags. I use the biggest eye-lags I can find—a ⅝-inch drop-forged type. Position them only about three or four feet above the desired height of the beam to reduce any possible swinging. Set a pilot hole in the tree using a bit ⅛ inch smaller than the eye-lag. Then screw the eye-lag into the hole using a lag spinner, if possible. A small crowbar will work too. As the tree grows, this bond will only get stronger.

Now cut a length of cable long enough to reach from your eye-lag to the beam.

Weave the short end of a preformed product called a Tree-Grip dead-end on to one end of the cable. The dead-ends are very easy to use and come in several different sizes. You can order them through your local arborist supply store. They come with instructions, so be sure to read about and fully understand how to use them.

Now thread the long end of your dead-end through the eye-lag, being sure that you have the piece called the thimble looped around the eye-lag. (The thimble is a horseshoe-shaped runner that the dead-end rests on. It protects the dead-end from chafing directly against the eye-lag when the tree or treehouse moves. Order thimbles separately, making sure to get the appropriate size.) Once the long end is threaded through the eye-lag, weave it onto the cable to close the dead-end loop.

Now you can attach the other end of your cable to the beam, using another dead-end. Remember that the first end of your beam usually does not have to be set at any exact spot. You'll be able to level the beam and determine its final positioning when you hang the other end.

First loop a heavy chain twice around the beam at the point where the EHS cable hangs down. Make sure a couple of feet of beam extend out beyond that point. Bring the chain up to where the lower dead-end will thread through it, to determine the length of the cable. Cut your cable to that length and weave on the second dead-end in the same way you did the first one. When taking the cable measurement, make sure to include the length of that lower dead-end. *Never ever* shorten the length of the dead-ends, as doing so greatly reduces their holding power.

Release the line holding the cabled end of the beam up, so that the whole weight of the beam is now resting on the cable. Now position yourself at the other end of the beam. Bring a level with you, and have someone on the ground adjust the beam and tie it off when level.

Sink the next eye-lag in its predetermined branch so the cable drops down to attach at least two feet in from the end of the beam. Attach the upper dead-end just as you did on the other side. Wrap the heavy chain around the beam twice, as before, and raise up the two ends of chain to get the cable measurement. Now, go ahead and cut your cable, and weave the short end of the dead-end onto it. Then thread the long end of the dead-end through the chain and weave it onto the cable, making sure to use the thimble. Release the line holding the beam up. If the beam isn't sitting level, simply hoist it up again, unweave the lower dead-end and snip the cable the distance necessary to get the beam level. Reweave the dead-end onto the cable and

**A suspended point load foundation in progress.**

lower away. Sometimes a come-along positioned just above the beam is helpful in making these smaller beam adjustments. Big beams can easily weigh a few hundred pounds or more. A come-along set a few feet higher than the beam will allow you to comfortably adjust the level of the beam from your position in the tree. Once you have your cable measured for length, it's nice to give the come-along a few cranks to take some of the tension out of your work. When you have the dead-ends closed, back off the come-along and see how you did. The manufacturer of Tree-Grip dead-ends suggests you use a new dead-end if you need to adjust more than three times.

     Now when you go to attach additional beams, use this first beam as your level guide. I move to other positions in the tree or group of trees by using a long, straight 2 × 4 that I turn on edge to span to my next beam location. With a level on the 2 × 4, I determine where the next beam will be positioned on the next branch or trunk and go from there.

It's worth noting here that I often weave the short end of the Tree-Grip onto a length of cable that I precut while on the ground. Often when you are in the tree setting the first cables, you are not in an ideal position to be doing this work. Like everything in treehouse construction, try to do as much as you can on the ground. For this same reason I like to thread thimbles to the eye-lags on the ground as well.

One final note: Sometimes with larger treehouses you're stuck with spans of 16 feet or more that exceed comfortable load capacities. To avoid having to install heavy, oversized beams, or in some cases steel I-beams, I would not hesitate even for a moment to post down to the ground in midspan. Call me a treehouse traitor, but I don't care. I might even respond, "I know you are but what am I?" until you blast me with your pneumatic nail gun. You'll see why as I explain this simple posting procedure when we revisit Gus Gunther's treehouse up in Clam Gulch (see Chapter 7).

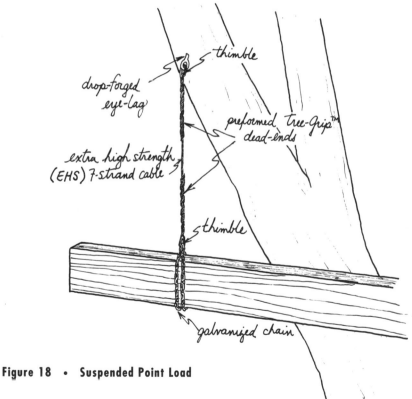

**Figure 18  •  Suspended Point Load**

Methods of Attachment

If the idea of these fancy Tree-Grip dead-ends doesn't thrill you, it is also possible to simply use heavy-duty stud cable and good old-fashioned cable clamps. Be sure to use at least two clamps at each splice if you use this method.

How you attach to your tree(s) is critical to your treehouse's stability. Again, your tree(s) will help you decide which attachment method, or combination, makes the most sense for your treehouse.

4

# Thinking Bigger

## Design

**T**reehouses are inherently the most fanciful structures that, as adults, we could ever dream of designing. While safe design is of utmost concern, we are nonetheless freed of most conventional building codes in treehouse construction and we can thereby let our imaginations run wild. The sky is literally the limit. (See page 59 for permitting information.)

While treehouses surely must be considered architecture, I imagine them often as sculpture. The one word of advice that I can give, outside of being sure your structural beams and joists are properly sized, is to pay attention to proportions. Part of what makes design one of my favorite aspects of a project is the challenge of coming up with an effective floor plan that fits the tree or trees that the house will be in. More often than not that means crunching things down in scale to the most minimal tolerances. It is very easy to overwhelm a tree with a house that is out of scale. Get out a piece of ¼-inch graph paper and try to sketch what comes into your thoughts. Your intuitive sense will tell you what looks good proportionally, so let that

*Photo at top of page:* **Michael Garnier, treehouse pioneer, relaxing in his hotel treehouse near Cave Junction, Oregon.**

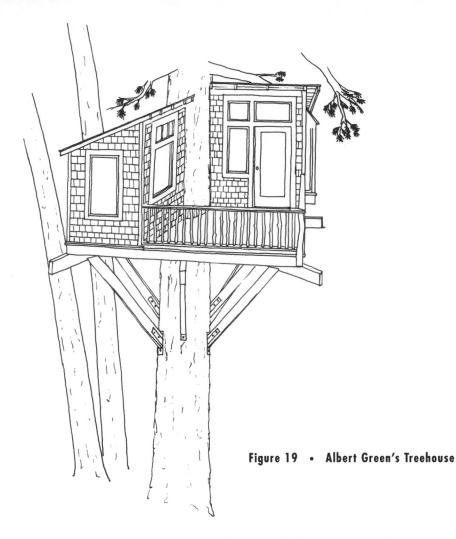

**Figure 19 • Albert Green's Treehouse**

speak to you. Get out your tape measure and physically "lay out" your dimensions on the floor. If you have a free corner in your house, do your layout from there to give you a better feel for where the walls actually will be. See what your tolerances actually are. I try to relate treehouse spaces to small boat spaces because they are similar in many ways. If you are looking to maximize your space, bring the house down low in the tree and spread your floor plan out. Even with large trees, however, I find it difficult to load anything more than 250 to 300 square feet in a tree without destroying the sense of scale. If you need more space than that, you can always build in pods of two or more buildings.

Another thing I do is drop my wall heights. If I use a flat ceiling I frame my walls to 7 feet. If I have an open ceiling I will try to bring my outside walls down even further where I don't have the conflict of a door. (Doors need at least 6 feet 6 inches of vertical space so you can allow for a 2 × 4 header and room for an adult to comfortably fit through without having to crawl.)

I suppose it would be possible to build a treehouse the size of a regular house, but the problem would be that once you were inside you'd risk forgetting that you are in a tree at all. By keeping things small you will always be close to the branches that lured you into the trees in the first place.

## Permitting

The treehouse skirts the edge of permitting law in the United States. The very nature of the structure—its reputation, its obscurity—has kept the issue out of mainstream discussion. After all, when you were a kid, did you seek a permit from your local zoning board to build your treefort? Well, neither do most adults. But if they did today they'd probably find out that the Uniform Building Code says treehouses are not "permit-able" structures, since they don't have traditional concrete foundations. So why are people continuing to build treehouses—sometimes very elaborate ones—every day? In my ten years in the treehouse world I haven't met anyone who's abandoned a project because his or her county wouldn't grant a permit. People ignore the permit issue for the same reasons they wanted to get off the ground in the first place—to find reprieve from the world of bureaucracy and regulation. Also, most treehouses are so small that they don't attract official attention anyway.

There are some permit exemptions, however, depending on where you live. Often, if the structure is less than 125 square feet, you won't need a permit. The only catch is that *no part* of the structure can exceed a height of 10 feet from the ground. In Oregon you can get a permit to build a treehouse, but the structure must be able to support at least 40 pounds per square foot of live load (people, animals). This is easy to meet; the problem rises from a wind-loading requirement that the structure must meet. Usually the requirement is an ability to withstand a sustained 80-mph wind. That is a toughie for treehouses—not because the structures are unsound, but because it is hard to measure the capacity to resist wind of a moving, organic structure. If a treehouse were to blow down in a windstorm, the local government doesn't want to be responsible.

Around the country treehouse owners are figuring out how to coexist with au-

**Michael Garnier will to go the mat in defense of his treehouses.**

thorities. One treehouse owner/activist, Michael Garnier, of Cave Junction, Oregon, is currently fighting in court to have his treehouse classified as a temporary structure, which would effectively exempt him from the wind-load requirement. Another idea he is exploring is to teach classes in treehouse philosophy and construction in his own treehouse, since apparently Oregon has less restrictive zoning requirements for schools. His operation, the Out 'n' About Treehouse Institute and Treesort, has classified itself as a school in the hopes of preserving its right to exist. In his case, things have unfortunately gotten a little ugly. The county has been doing all it can to have his eight treehouses removed. But it looks like some resolution is near, and I believe it will pave the way for a new understanding that all treehouse people will benefit from. Michael's first treehouse was on the cover of my book *Treehouses!* (The county was already after him then, in case you want to know.)

If you are curious or worried, I suggest contacting your local building department to see what their rules and attitudes are. Whether you pursue a permit or not, you can at least play it safer by building your treehouse solidly and at a low height and using multiple trees to support it. That way the chances of the wind coming along and blowing the whole structure over are reduced, making it harder for the permit people to build a clear case against you.

If you want to avoid the issue altogether, you might decide to build in a secluded area, not readily visible from the road. If that's not possible, go to your neighbors and show them your plans; nine times out of ten they're the ones who'll turn you in. If they don't have a problem, you've cleared a big hurdle.

Chances are good that you'll have no problems. From my own experience, I can tell you that most zoning boards don't even want to know about treehouses. Why? Because if they go after you, they'd have to go after every kids' treehouse in town. It'd be a public relations nightmare. Likewise, hundreds of people have built treehouses without even being aware of the permit issue, or in defiance of what they see as an unbending bureaucracy. Ultimately the decision to build or not is yours.

Now, let's get back to the things you *can* do—like learning about a man who took a great leap . . . upward . . . with a vacation home in a ponderosa pine!

# 5

# A Vacation Spot in the Air

**When Albert Green bought the old Gibbs ranch in Pleas-**
ant Valley, Montana, he knew he was getting a good deal: thirty-five acres with a
working barn, work shed, a 126-year-old farmhouse, lakefront property, a couple of
stands of old-growth ponderosa, and the quirky, luxurious distinction of being the
last house on the power grid (the last telephone pole in Pleasant Valley stands across
the road from his place).

The road that runs past the property—the only one in the entire part of the
state—is a regrade of the abandoned Burlington-Northern railway. As you drive the
dirt and gravel lane, signs of the old rail line appear now and again—a piece of crum-
bling trestle off in a marsh, a pile of railroad ties just off the shoulder of the road, or,
as on Albert's ranch, tree-markings where the Indians taught railroad engineers how
to tap sap during the winter months.

"That's what finally sold me on the place," says the 32-year-old self-employed
Seattleite. "The sense of history here is breathtaking. From my ranch I look down
Pleasant Valley, where earlier this century the Native Americans hunted deer, elk,
bear, and cougar. It's amazing. There are signs everywhere of their presence." In fact,

---

*Photo at top of page:* **A guideline helps steady wall on its ascent.**

the small knoll 250 yards from the main house—the site of the ponderosa stand that holds Albert's new treehouse—was once a temporary campsite for the local Indians as they passed through the valley in pursuit of game.

As Albert spent time at his new ranch over the first year, fixing it up and adjusting to the big sky and the solitude, one particular ponderosa tree began to catch his eye. It stands straight as an arrow, 180 feet tall and 14 feet around at its base, with two smaller pines nearby as kind of ladies-in-waiting. From Albert's porch the majestic pine seems to lord over the surrounding hills. One day, while eating breakfast on the porch, Albert suddenly thought, Wouldn't it be great to build a treehouse in that tree? Two years later, he did it.

Albert and I had met a couple of years earlier while I was building a treehouse for a mutual friend on Salt Spring Island, British Columbia. One day in August 1995, he called and invited me out to the Montana ranch—under the pretense, he later admitted, to build him a covered wraparound porch. While I was out there he casually sprung his idea on me. He knew I'd fall in love with the tree. He was right; I'd noticed it even before he brought it up. We put down our tools and walked across the open fields to the ponderosa.

The three-tree stand was perfect. The main tree could easily support an umbrella-style foundation, and the two smaller pines could be used for extra support if necessary (it turned out not to be). Also, the branch line was at least forty feet up, meaning we could really go high with this one if we wanted to (boy, did we).

"I've got a lot of extra lumber," he said, looking at me, then at the tree, "if you've got some extra time."

"When were you thinking?" I asked.

"How about next summer?" Albert said.

I looked up again. For a split second I could see the finished house, the bay window in place, the cedar shingles, the galvanized metal roof that would match the one on his new porch, Albert sitting on the front deck, his feet up, watching the sky.

"Next summer," I said. "Let's do it."

The following July, Albert and I assembled a small work crew of motley and not so motley helpers. Two weeks later the job was done. The following section goes into great detail on the specific construction of Albert's treehouse. We take treehouse building to a higher level than in the first example of the kids' treehouse, but the basic principles are still the same.

Before we move on I want to mention a couple of things about the Montana project. First, Albert's treehouse is a bigger undertaking than the kids' treehouse. There are several differences in construction and approach to building that you'll notice right away.

For one, a lot of initial work took place with me and my crew dangling from safety lines instead of standing on the ground. This happened mainly while we were securing the foundation to the tree. Albert's foundation is an umbrella foundation, so called because the beams fan out from the trunk like the ribs of a parasol. The tree rises right up through the center of the treehouse and disappears through the roof. While the foundation was coming together there was nothing for us to stand on, but with our secure safety lines, backup safety lines, and arborist-tested climbing techniques, we were completely safe. It took some of us a few minutes to adjust to the vulnerable feeling of hanging 30 feet off the ground, but we all got used to it in no time.

Also, the general materials are heavier and less easy to maneuver. They require more complex ways of hauling components into the tree. For the most part we relied on a block and tackle and pulleys.

What's the same about this treehouse and the kids'? For one, the basic principles of building. Those never change, from measuring and cutting 2 × 4s to sinking nails to painting the interior. The same procedures that saw us through the kids' treehouse will see us through here.

This project also has a similarly huge fun quotient. We had a blast putting this thing together, hanging out for two weeks in the Montana wild, eating well, working hard, laughing a lot, drooling. Any treehouse brings this out in the builder.

Finally, the very same wood butchers who built the kids' treehouse cobbled this prizewinner together. It's just bigger and higher up in the tree, which requires more time and patience. So don't sweat it. The time issue is taken care of, since there's really no such thing as time. And once you know this, patience becomes second nature. But . . .

## Safety First

Treehouse projects must begin with safety. Initially, that means setting and securing all of the safety lines, pulleys, and blocks and tackle you'll need to complete the job with minimum risk to yourself and your crew (if you're lucky enough to have a crew). It also means setting some basic ground rules. No work site is ever 100 percent safe, but there are several things you can do to minimize risk of injury to the folks on and around the site.

Make it absolutely clear to everyone on the site—from workers to family to visiting friends and curious neighbors—that *walking under the tree is forbidden during construction.* Obviously, once in a while someone will have to venture below the treehouse, like when you're hoisting the walls up or if something falls that you need to retrieve. I recommend requiring hard hats for everyone near the perimeter of the tree; even the best builder drops tools now and then. If there are kids around, under no circumstances should they be allowed close to the building area. Between the dangerous tools and possible falling objects, it's just too risky. If you want to include them, find off-site tasks to keep them busy, like the nailing exercise I mentioned in Chapter 2. Also, think of errands they can do, like serving as runners between the site and the kitchen. There's nothing like looking down from the tree to see a gaggle of kids approaching with plates of sandwiches and cold iced tea.

Whenever anyone's in the tree, they've got to be wearing a safety line attached properly to a climbing harness. This is one of the most important and strongly enforced rules around my projects.

## Talk to the Tree

**B**efore I set my lines in the tree I like to take a few minutes to hold an informal ceremony. I do this for every treehouse, because the host of the treehouse is a living creature. I know it sounds crazy, but what I like to do is place a hand on the tree so that I can feel the energy that the tree is emitting. At this point you can make up any ceremony you wish. I like to ask permission to use the tree. I promise to be careful and to treat the tree with respect and then I explain my intentions. After these brief words and a few moments, I bury a clove of garlic at the base of the trunk to symbolically ward off disease and evil spirits. Whatever you do, even if you do nothing at all, it's up to you. But approaching the project respectfully will surely mean less damage done, and a healthier tree/treehouse relationship.

## Your Lines Are Your Friends

Setting your first safety line in the tree is often an imposing task, particularly in a tree like Albert's, in which the first branch did not start for 40 feet. Call in an arborist if you are the least bit uncomfortable in setting this first line. If you have access to a 30- to 40-foot extension ladder, that is a good way to get a start. Be warned, however—ladders are downright dangerous, particularly so when used on uneven ground and leaning against a round tree trunk. They make me very nervous. At Albert's I climbed on a ladder as far as I felt comfortable and then tossed a small nylon line with a weight on the end over the closest large branch. It took a few tosses but we were then able to catch the end and tie that to a climbing rope and pull it back over. On the ground I put on my climbing harness (recently I bought a tree-climbing saddle, which I strongly recommend) and tied the all-important climber's knot. This is a wonderful self-hoisting system that relies on a self-locking friction knot. All arborists use it in one form or another to get up and down trees.

Modern climbing ropes are made of a polypropylene blend. They need to be a minimum of $\frac{1}{2}$ inch thick and have a tensile strength of at least 5,400 pounds. There are two styles of climbing rope: three-strand and braided. I prefer braided because it's more flexible and feels better in your hands. Some say it even holds a knot better. Don't skimp on your rope.

Before I describe the workings of the climber's knot, let me start by giving an overview of the basic types of rigging that I use when building treehouses. There are two groups of lines to use: safety lines and hauling lines. Of the safety lines I will first describe the climber's line and the all-important climber's knot. I next describe static safety lines and the associ-

**Figure 20  •  Bowline Knot**

**Here is the knot where the rabbit comes out of the hole, goes around the tree, and goes back into the hole. It's a simple and essential knot that is easy to tie, can take a huge strain, and unties easily.**

ated loop Prusik knot. Of the hauling lines there are two types: block and tackle and the standard single pulley. I will also show all of the pertinent knots that go along with rigging. There are only a few and they are easy.

The lines are crucial to having your project run smoothly. They are also the most important element in keeping safe, so be sure you get familiar with your rope and each knot before you try it in the field.

## SAFETY LINES AND THE CLIMBER'S KNOT

The lines you use to haul yourself up and down are called climbing lines, and they use a "climber's knot." We use these lines and knots primarily at the beginning of a project when we are building the structural framework. Once you are comfortable with this knot, you will be able to go places you have never even dreamed of.

**The climber's knot.**

I like to set my climbing lines 10 to 15 feet above where I plan to work. Loop your line over a strong parent branch on the main tree trunk (see Figure 21) at the appropriate height. Tie one end of this line to your climbing harness with a small bowline knot. Leave about 4 to 5 feet loose and hanging in front of you. Essentially you have two lines— the line rising from your safety belt and the line running down from the tree. The lines get tied together with a climber's knot using the short section hanging in front of you. Pulling on the loose end of the rope raises you up. It's not as hard as it might

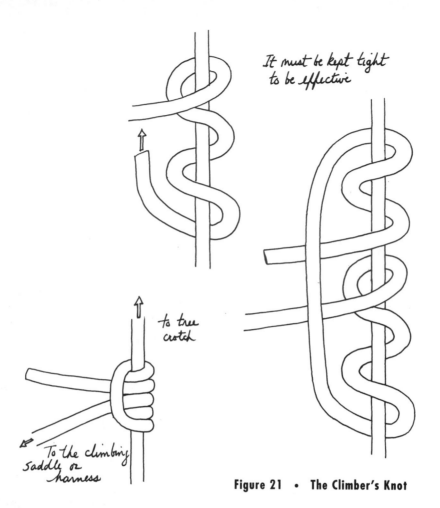

It must be kept tight to be effective

to tree crotch

To the climbing saddle or harness

**Figure 21 • The Climber's Knot**

sound: You cinch your way up and anchor yourself at the new height by sliding the climber's knot up to take up the slack in the line attached to your harness. Getting down is even easier—just loosen the knot with one hand by squeezing it, and let yourself slide down in a controlled manner. If you feel as if you're dropping too fast, pull the tail of the climber's knot and you'll slow down. I like to set at least three climbing lines around a tree so we don't have to keep moving them as we work around a tree. I do the same in multitree structures so we can move from line to line as needed. For an added measure of comfort when working between lines, it is a good idea to hook into two lines at once. Tree workers often carry a second safety line called a lanyard, which adjusts to fit around the tree where you are working and hooks into a second set of rings (called D-rings) that all tree-climbing saddles have on the sides. It gives an important added measure of safety and I recommend using one. With the self-hoisting system ready, you can set the remaining ropes you need to get the treehouse built.

Some of the safety lines are static. That is to say, they don't move. This second type of safety line keeps you safe while working from the platform up in the tree. We set three static safety lines that we use after the platform is built and can stand freely in the tree. I set each static safety line by wrapping a rope around the tree trunk twice and tying it off with a bowline knot. The remainder of the rope hangs down to the ground. If you leave it short, be sure to tie a figure-eight knot at the bitter end. From this point on, anyone on the platform during construction is required to tie off to one of these lines with a loop Prusik hooked independently to their safety harness (see Figure 23). I've found old, discarded 1-inch crab lines to be inexpensive and more than strong enough for the static safety lines. They're as tough as they come and great for our purposes. If you don't live anywhere near a fishing community, maybe there's another source of strong, secondhand line to look into.

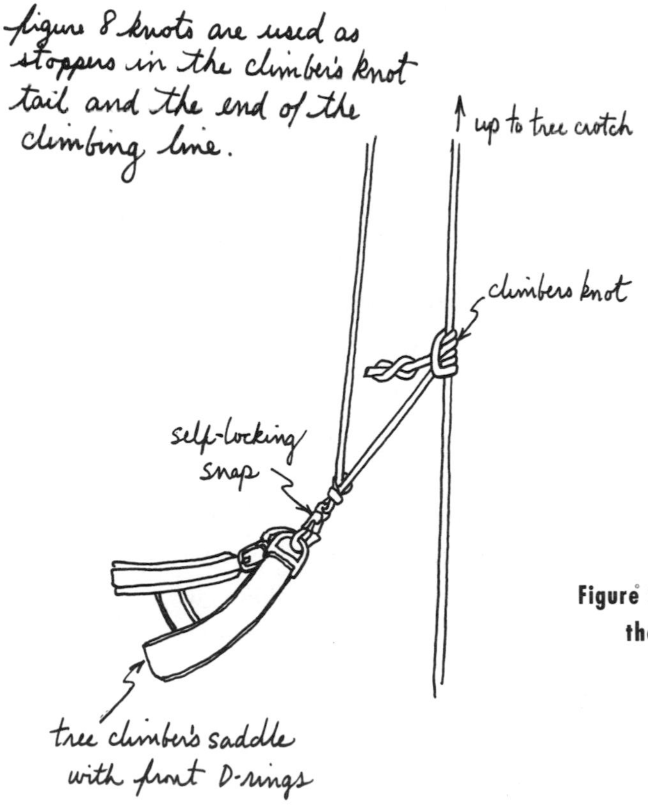

figure 8 knots are used as stoppers in the climber's knot tail and the end of the climbing line.

↑ up to tree crotch

climbers knot

self-locking snap

tree climber's saddle with front D-rings

**Figure 22  •  Tying in with the Climber's Knot**

A Vacation Spot in the Air

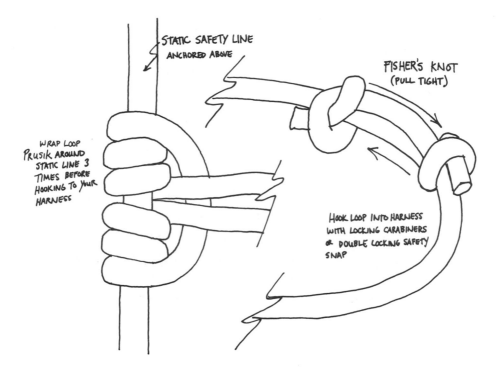

STATIC SAFETY LINE
ANCHORED ABOVE

FISHER'S KNOT
(PULL TIGHT)

WRAP LOOP
PRUSIK AROUND
STATIC LINE 3
TIMES BEFORE
HOOKING TO YOUR
HARNESS

HOOK LOOP INTO HARNESS
WITH LOCKING CARABINERS
& DOUBLE LOCKING SAFETY
SNAP

**Figure 23 • Loop Prusik Knot**

### HAULING LINES

For hauling, I use a block and tackle for the heavy lifting and a few single pulleys for everything else. Before setting any of these lines, you'll need to figure out where the roofline of your treehouse is. In the case of the Montana treehouse, we'd decided the crown of the roof would be at 40 feet, where the branch line begins. Then we went up another 10 or 20 feet beyond that point. That's where we attached most of our lines. I've found that the long distance gives more play as you work around the tree.

First set up your block and tackle. This is going to be the workhorse of all your lines. It's important to keep it from tangling up in itself, so try and choose a spot where branches won't interfere with the lines. Rig the block and tackle on the ground. Find a very sturdy branch to tie off to. At Albert's we had it positioned above the porch so we could easily haul up the walls and other heavy items onto an unobstructed part of the house platform.

Next, tie off your pulley line to a secure branch. I use my pulley as a movable device, since it's easier to move and reset than the block and tackle. Its mobility was especially helpful as we moved around the tree, hoisting the beams for Albert's foundation. I usually set this pulley 10 to 15 feet above the platform height. Once I am in the tree, I use one final line to haul my tools and material up and down—a milk crate tied to a line works well here.

Okay—Step One done. All lines secure! Back to Earth!

## The Foundation

**W**hat's holding this thing up anyway? As I've already mentioned, the Gibbs treehouse has an "umbrella foundation." This is really a fixed point load system arranged around one tree in a way that resembles the framework of an umbrella. To support the beams of the

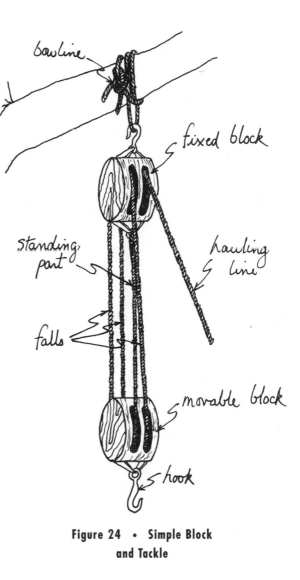

**Figure 24 • Simple Block and Tackle**

platform, it uses knee braces supported by customized brackets bolted into the tree. The beams themselves are also set in brackets, similar to the knee brace brackets. It is critically important to space the knee braces and beams evenly and levelly. That means setting your upper (beam) brackets and lower (knee brace) brackets plumb and perfectly in relation to each other. If you're not exact on this part, you'll run into trouble as the structural framework goes up. Trust me; on Albert's house we ran into

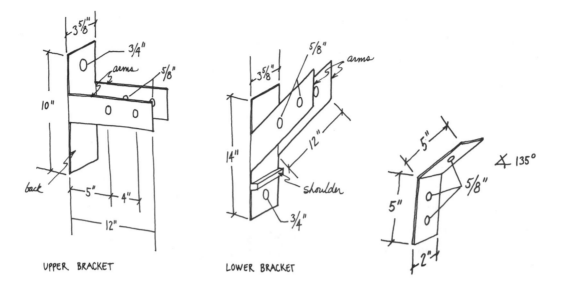

UPPER BRACKET    LOWER BRACKET

**Figure 25 • Customized Manufactured 1/4-inch Steel Brackets**

**Figure 26 • Angle Bracket**

**Brackets are held by a single bolt. In Albert's situation we used one ¾-inch-thick by 10-inch-long galvanized lag bolt in each bracket to support the weight of the treehouse. An engineer might consider this size bolt overkill, but I like to err on the side of safety when I am 30 feet up a tree.**

this very problem setting the fourth beam. It would not align properly because the upper and lower brackets were slightly off—in relation to each other and on the vertical plane—and we spent hours trying to determine and then solve the problem. This will become clearer in a minute.

## Setting the Brackets

The first step in building the foundation is setting your brackets. Hoist yourself into the tree and measure the circumference of the tree at the height at which you'll set the brackets that anchor the beams. In Albert's case we were about 30 feet off the ground. If you've got a ladder against the tree, use it to get yourself as high as possible, sliding your climbing knot up as you climb. We had only a 24-foot ladder, so when we couldn't go any higher, we stepped off the ladder and hoisted ourselves from there. That's a lot less tiring than hoisting yourself up all the way from the ground.

Use your level to make sure your circumference measurement is accurate. A water level would be perfect for

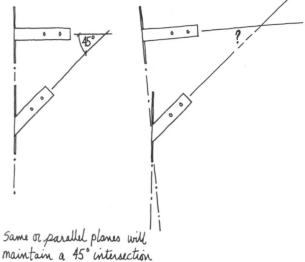

*Same or parallel planes will maintain a 45° intersection*

**Figure 27 • Planes of Brackets, Right and Wrong**

this job, but we got by using a standard 2-foot level by holding it against the tree and steadily wrapping it around and keeping a close eye on the bubble to make sure it stayed as close to level as possible. Next, divide the tree's circumference by the number of brackets you have—in this case, eight. Set a temporary nail in the bark at each of the points.

The process is now fairly simple. You'll attach the upper brackets first, one at a time, and use each successive one to level the next as you work your way around the tree. Run a level from each bracket to the next as

**Milk crates make ideal tool holders when installing brackets.**

A Vacation Spot in the Air

you proceed. We could move around about a quarter of the tree by swinging on our climbing lines and gaining toeholds in the bark. Eventually we had to move our lines to new branches.

To make sure each bracket rests plumb against the tree (that is, perpendicular to the ground) you'll have to take an adze or hatchet to the bark and carve out a plumb surface against which the brackets will set. If you need to do any carving, be careful not to remove too much bark. If you cut too deeply you'll injure the tree. You don't need to go very deep, just deep enough to make the surface plumb. I recommend an eight-inch torpedo level to ensure you've got it. It's easy to carry and fits into the space you've carved out. If the upper and lower brackets aren't all plumb they'll send the knee braces and beams off at inconsistent angles, and your foundation won't come together properly.

Now you're ready to actually attach the upper brackets. Since you're going to need several tools for this part, I recommend putting them all in a milk crate and hoisting the crate up with your pulley. By the way, I rely heavily on electric power tools for these projects. A treehouse would take ten times as long to put together if done by hand—just like a ground house. If you don't have access to power, I suggest you rent a generator. The drone of a generator certainly interrupts the tranquility of the scene, but it speeds up the building process immensely.

To attach the upper brackets you'll need:

*¾ × 10-in. galvanized lag bolts with washers (8)*

*impact wrench with 1⅛-in. socket*

*level*

*¼-in. custom-manufactured steel brackets (8)*

*½-in. drill with ⅝ × 10-in. auger (for setting pilot holes)*

*1 plumb line*

Set yourself back up in the tree. Take your auger and drill the pilot hole for the first upper bracket's bolt. Again, be sure the surface is leveled before drilling the hole. Next, set the bracket against the tree and sink the bolt into the tree using an impact wrench. This should be fairly easy with the electric tools. If you don't have an impact wrench, a ratchet will work. Move around the tree repeating the procedure until all eight brackets are in, double-checking the level as you go.

With all your upper brackets in, it is time to concentrate on preparing your horizontal 4 × 8 beams. Rather than taking the time and mental energy to figure each beam's precise length, I cut them long. You can always go back and trim them after they're attached. I actually prefer the look of beams that don't all match each other in length. For me it gives the treehouse a rougher look, without compromising structural integrity. The extra length also provides a handy place to set scaffolding for future window cleaning.

## Preparing the Beams

There are eight beams, four long ones on the corners and four shorter ones in between. After predrilling all the bracket holes for the ⅝-inch through-bolts, I cut a ½-inch notch into the lower side of the beams into which the knee brace will set. On

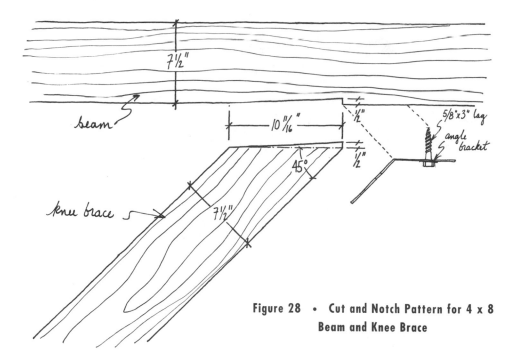

**Figure 28 • Cut and Notch Pattern for 4 x 8 Beam and Knee Brace**

A Vacation Spot in the Air

the short beams I cut that notch at 5 feet out; on the longer beams I cut it at 6 feet. I also attach the ¼-inch steel angle bracket that secures the connection of the beam and knee brace (see Figure 28). It's got a 135-degree angle and attaches to the beam with one bolt, so you can pivot it out of the way when you set the knee brace.

## Setting the Lower Brackets

While someone is precutting the beams, someone else can be up in the tree setting the lower brackets. Remember, you want a 45-degree angle between the knee brace and the beam and between the knee brace and the tree. (The tree, the beam, and the

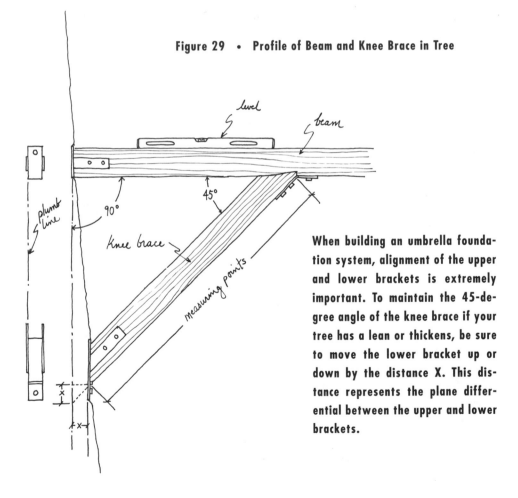

**Figure 29  •  Profile of Beam and Knee Brace in Tree**

When building an umbrella foundation system, alignment of the upper and lower brackets is extremely important. To maintain the 45-degree angle of the knee brace if your tree has a lean or thickens, be sure to move the lower bracket up or down by the distance X. This distance represents the plane differential between the upper and lower brackets.

knee brace form an isosceles triangle.) To achieve this, set the lower brackets 5 feet down from the upper brackets for the shorter beams. This is the same distance as the distance between the tree and the notch on those beams. For the longer beams set the lower brackets 6 feet down from the upper brackets, which is the distance between the tree and the notch on the longer beams.

This part is a little tricky because you've got to compensate for any curve or thickening in the tree trunk. To see whether there's a differential, set a plumb line from an arm of an installed upper bracket and let the plumb bob dangle down to the rough point marked 5 or 6 feet below on the bark. If there's a distance between the back of the bracket and where the plumb line crosses the arm of the bracket, you'll need to move your lower bracket up by that distance. If the tree leans in the other direction, drop the lower bracket by the distance measured from the plumb bob back to the tree.

Carve the seat for the lower brackets just as you did for the upper brackets. Make sure the carved seat is set plumb with the upper bracket, and that it's on a parallel plane. Attach the brackets using the auger and impact wrench, just as with the upper brackets. Again, if you don't get this right, the upper and lower brackets will guide the beam and knee brace to different end points. They won't meet up where they're supposed to.

## Setting the Beams

Your beams are ready to be hoisted into the tree. We did this one at a time, starting with a short beam. Using a bowline knot and double wrapping for security, raise the beam on the pulley. Make sure to tie the rope just outside the center of the beam so that you can maneuver the outside end up or down once you've bolted the beam to the tree.

For setting the beams you'll need one or two people on the ground hoisting and, if possible, two people in the tree. The beam is held into the bracket by two 5/8-inch through-bolts. Once you've set the beam in its bracket and set the two bolts, lower or raise the beam until it's level. Hold it there. Measure the distance from the outside edge of the beam notch down to the shoulder of the lower bracket. Write that number down; it's the length of that particular knee brace. No two knee braces

**Installing the beams and knee braces on the Montana treehouse proved to be tricky business. Ropes and safety lines were a critical part of this phase.**

will be exactly the same length, so the best way to avoid confusing them is to cut and attach each knee brace as you set each beam.

Have the ground crew cut the eight knee braces. We used 4 × 8s to match the beams. The bottom edge of the knee brace should be cut at a 45-degree angle, but remember that at the top you have to compensate for the notch. So, instead of cutting a 45-degree angle, I just mark the 45-degree line with a pencil. Then, on the sharp point where the line intersects the edge of the 4 × 8, I mark a 90-degree angle ½ inch up on the 4 × 8—the depth of the notch. I draw my cut line from that point back down to the other end of the original 45-degree line. Now you can make the cut and send the knee brace aloft.

Raise the knee braces with the rope slightly to the outside of center, just as you did with the beams. Wedge the outside end snugly up into the notch in the beam and push the inside end into the lower bracket so it's resting on the shoulder.

This might take some wriggling, but it should slip in without too much trouble. If all looks good, drill your two holes in the knee brace and set your two through-bolts now. Go slow as you drill and make sure you're drilling completely straight, so the bit comes out matching the hole on the other side of the bracket. Now turn back to the notch and drill the holes for the $\frac{5}{8} \times 3$-inch angle bracket lag bolts. Screw them in. This makes for some exciting aerial work, and helps you appreciate an electric impact wrench if you're not using one.

Got it done? Great—just seven more to go. When all the beams and knee braces are in place you can lower yourself down and take a break. Your foundation has been founded!

## The Floor

**Y**ou've got the eight beams and knee braces attached to the tree. If your treehouse is high off the ground, like Albert's, you undoubtedly felt a bit nervous dangling from a line as you drilled, measured, and leveled. Well, now you can take heart in knowing the next step is putting down the floor—you know, that three-quarters of an inch between you and Earth that you can stand on without getting vertigo. It's important, and once it's in, it feels like a luxury.

### Setting the Floor Joists

The floor joists are the horizontal framing members that sit on edge and span across the beams. Your floor is nailed to the floor joists. This section describes the process of installing floor joists 30 feet from the ground on beams $3\frac{1}{2}$ inches wide. Make sure you are properly tied on!

To help get things roughly square, start by nailing together the rim joists—the boards that run along the perimeter of the beams and form the outside rim of the floor frame. The rim joists—in fact, the whole floor frame—rests on top of the beams. For this part, 2 × 6s work well because our longest spans were only 7 feet. Albert's treehouse is 13 by 14 feet so we cut the two longer rim joists to 14 feet exactly (see Figure 30). Mark them every two feet on center so you'll know where to attach the intermediate floor joists later. The two shorter rim joists or end joists fit inside

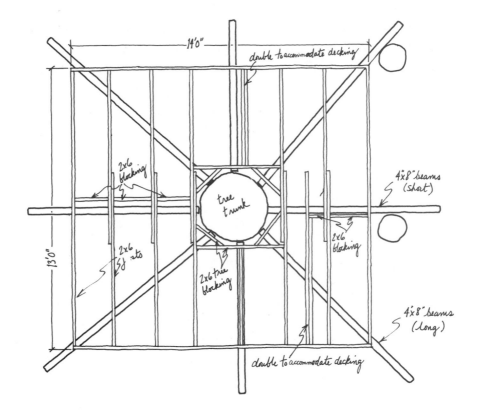

Figure 30 • Foundation and Floor Framing Plan

the longer ones, so they should be cut to 12 feet 9 inches to compensate for the 1½-inch width of each of the longer rim joists. This will give you a net of 13 feet in that direction.

Nail the rim joists together where they meet at the corners with four 16-penny framing nails—from the 14-footers into the 12-foot-9-inchers. I don't worry about getting the floor frame perfectly square at this time. Let the factory-cut plywood flooring do that for you when you're ready. At this time I jockey the frame around so that it looks square enough to the eye (and also finds its position relative to the beams and the two satellite trees on the north edge of the platform).

The floor frame is ready for the floor joists. Because we didn't have enough long 2 × 6s for the five intermediate, full-length floor joists, we used eight-footers that Albert had stored in his shop, and sistered them up to span the distance. You've already marked the 14-foot rim joists every 2 feet. Now nail the floor joists to the rim joists with four 16-penny galvanized sinkers. Nail from the outside through the rim joists into the ends of the floor joists. As you'll see, your work will soon be blocked by the tree trunk. You'll have to cut those center joists short to compensate for it. First box in the trunk with 2 × 6 joist material from the two nearest complete joists, crossing within three or four inches of the trunk. That boxing acts as blocking and will support the shortened joists (see Figure 30).

Now you have the entire floor frame nailed together but still resting freely on the beams. It's time to square it up and nail it down. Once again, adjust the floor frame where you want it to lie on the frame. This doesn't have to be exact, since your beams run long on all sides. But you've also boxed in the trunk now, so you don't have too much play. With the pulley, raise a piece of ¾ × 4 × 8 tongue-and-groove plywood into the tree and lay it down on the southeast corner of the frame. With luck you will drop it in place and find everything perfectly square already. If not, adjust the rim joists so they run flush with the edge of the plywood on both the 4-foot and 8-foot sides. I don't recommend this method for large buildings, but for small structures this effectively squares up your frame. Toenail both outside edges of the rim joists where they cross the beams with 16-penny framing nails to secure that right angle. Now slide the plywood sheet out of the way and toenail the rim from the inside. You may also toenail your intermediate joists where they would be covered by the first sheet of plywood. Repeat this at the northeast corner and you should have all four corners squared. Now move your way across the frame and toenail all the floor joists where they cross the beams using the same 16-penny sinkers. We chose not to nail the joist to the two beams closest to the satellite trees on the north. We left those free so that if the young trees bump them in heavy wind they can give way a bit.

## Laying Down the Floor

Now you're ready to lay down the ¾-inch tongue-and-groove plywood floor. The tongue and groove is great because it adds support to the floor over the spaces where there is no joist. Without it you'd have to block underneath the seam for added support. We started flooring on the southeast corner.

Hoist the plywood up using the pulley. Run a line of subfloor glue on the joists where the first piece of plywood will lie. Lay down that first piece with the long grooved edge along the east edge of the rim joist. Nail it down using 10-penny galvanized or ring shank nails. When that edge is in, look to see that things remain square, and nail down the rest of the plywood sheet. To make it easier to hit the joists with my nails I snap a chalk line on the face of the plywood that marks the center of the joists running underneath.

Before nailing the second sheet of plywood along the east rim joist, we consulted the floor plan to see what was required. In Albert's case it called for plywood only in the spaces that were to be covered by enclosed spaces; the rest was to be decked with 2 × 6-inch cedar. The footprint of the enclosed area was 11 × 7 feet in this section of the treehouse, with the 11-foot dimension running along the east rim. This indicated an overall length for our second sheet of plywood of just 3 feet (11 feet minus the 8 feet of the first sheet already installed). Notice on the floor framing plan that an independent joist was installed to accommodate the butt end of this plywood at this uneven distance.

To complete this section of flooring go back to the south end of the platform and rip a piece of plywood (cut in the long dimension) to 3 feet wide. Be sure to take off the tongue side so the tongue and groove will fit properly. With this piece we ran into a situation common in treehouse construction: we needed to scribe a cut to fit around the tree trunk. For this, I like to leave about an inch of space between the bark and plywood. The following section describes how to properly scribe and cut this 3 × 8-foot sheet of plywood.

## SCRIBING

Scribing allows you to cut out the shape of the tree from your floor—and later, your walls and roof—allowing them to wrap nicely around the trunk. To me, this "meeting" is one of the most important design elements of the treehouse. The trunk, after all, is where your house and tree come together. It's the visible connection between man and nature. If it looks sloppy I feel somehow an injustice has been done.

Scribing is easy. You've laid down all the plywood you can in the 11 × 7-foot section. Now you've got a 3 × 8-foot length of plywood and the trunk to contend with. This is a good piece to practice scribing on since it will eventually be covered by the finished floor. Here's what you do.

From the northwest point of the first sheet of plywood you placed on the 2 × 6 floor framing, pull your tape back along the west edge and mark four points at 6-inch increments. Then take your tape and measure the distance 90 degrees off that edge of the plywood to the tree trunk. Write these distances down. Now go to your 3 × 8-foot sheet of plywood and, starting in the lower corner of the

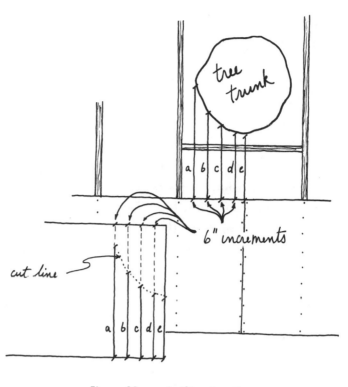

**Figure 31 • Scribing to a Tree**

female edge, make the same four marks by pulling your tape along the female edge and marking a point every 6 inches. Do the same on the opposite side and connect those points using a straightedge or chalk line. Using the measurements from your list, transfer the corresponding points onto the corresponding line on your 3 × 8-foot sheet of plywood. Circle or somehow highlight that point on your line. On your clean sheet you should now see an arc of points that mirrors the shape of the tree trunk. Connect the dots! That's the line you'll cut.

Blocking needs to be installed where the outer edges of your plywood floor spans the joists. Note in the floor plan where the plywood ends and be sure to add blocking. In the case of your 3 × 8-foot sheet that you just scribed, notice that on the west edge are spans between the joists that need blocking. Be sure to place that into the 2 × 6 floor framing before you nail down your carefully scribed piece. Now would be a good time to block for the bedroom section as well. Note on the floor plan and framing plan where the blocking goes. Now you are ready to finish the remaining plywood flooring in the bedroom section. You will have a few pieces to scribe, but I think you can handle it.

## THE DECKS

Now, all that is left to floor are the two decks. Both are made with 2 × 6 cedar planking with ³⁄₁₆-inch spacing—about the width of a 16-penny nail. The cedar is expensive but looks good and lasts a long time, even when exposed to the elements. If our joists had been set at 16-inch centers we would have used ⁵⁄₄ × 6 cedar, which is a bit lighter. But either one works just fine. The one consideration here is to install blocking to more easily accommodate the ends of the decking. You will notice in the floor framing plan that the two places where this comes in handy are the south end of the entry deck and the north end of the main deck. Since the decking on both decks runs north to south, this block provides an easier nailing surface than the ³⁄₄-inch space that typically remains when you split a 2 × 6 with the plywood flooring of the buildings' footprint.

## Insulating the Floor

Since we were in Montana, where even summer nights can freeze a wart off a hedgehog, I decided to insulate the floor. Albert had some 2-inch-thick, 2-foot-wide rigid foam insulation that worked perfectly. In order to have something to nail the finished floor to I had to install sleepers—2 × 1½-inch strips ripped from 2 × 4s—laid on edge and screwed to the floor. The idea is to form 2-foot-wide pockets in which the foam can sit. Later I set the walls directly on top of, and screwed them down into, those sleepers. When all the walls were up and the roof on, we went back and laid down the finished floor.

## The Frame Job

Treehouses are assembled in a very unconventional manner. As we mentioned when discussing the kids' treehouse, all of the exterior siding and trim is applied directly to the rough framing while the walls are still on the ground. When the sections are

Once the walls are screwed together, we begin installing windows.

With the trim painted dark green and cedar shingles left unpainted, the house fits naturally in the trees.

Plentiful spruce trees on Gus's property provided ideal beams for the treehouse foundation.

You can finish the interior of your treehouse to any level you wish. In this case we used old shiplap boards to panel the interior walls. The door and chair rail were left over from a previous building project.

The treehouse quickly takes form once the walls and windows are in place. Now it's time to put on the roof.

Sitting in the bay window seat is like sitting on a limb thirty feet off the ground.

Gus's elegant treehouse also appears to provide excellent dry storage for his many valuable items.

Hoisting the first wall to the plat-form. We tied a block and tackle to the bumper of a truck for the heavy lifting while two others on the ground helped guide the wall away from obstructions.

Having the tree as part of the interior gives Albert's house unique charm. It also provides the house with a constant flow of interesting bug life, as the tree serves as a major highway for many species of insects.

The temporary access door for Albert's treehouse proved to be more practical than the planned stairway. Since it's removable when Albert is away, the house is virtually impregnable.

In the summer, Charlie and Henry's treehouse will practically disappear in the tree's foliage. Treehouse building is actually easier on the tree in the winter months, when the tree is dormant.

Build railings long at the ends, then trim them to fit snugly when they are ready to be installed.

In roughly 10 days, with 260 hours of labor, Gus had a house he could call his own.

Site-built windows can save money but not time.

Let in as much light as possible, so you never forget that you are in the trees.

Simple, lightweight panels combine to form rigid walls.

My office does not look quite so organized
anymore.

Tranquility among the
towering firs.

The giants that
are the hosts of
Albert's house
seem no less alive
and inquisitive
than giraffes.

 Everything is big in Montana.

 Last wall.

 Make your railings safe and strong. It's not the fall that will kill you, it's the sudden stop at the end.

**Team photo snapped after Albert's platform is complete.**

hoisted into position there should be little, if any, work left on the outside of the building. Building the walls in this manner makes for quite a secure and stable structure, particularly when the roof is put on. After years of experimenting, I'm convinced my wall frames are sound. One reassuring statistic: None of them have ever fallen apart or blown over.

Build the walls on the ground. Build them so that everything screws together. Up in the tree the framing comes together in segments, with each panel connecting to the next. Because each new piece depends on the piece set before it, always think ahead to how the connections work, especially at the corners. I visualized Albert's treehouse as two rectangular boxes, similar to the small treehouse we built for Charlie and Henry, that overlap on one corner. The living room section is a 7 × 11-foot box and the bedroom is a 6 × 7-foot box. To keep things consistent, I decided to designate all of the long walls in the two boxes as by-walls and all of the short walls as butt-walls. The longer sides of the two boxes will run their full lengths of 7 and 11 feet

A Vacation Spot in the Air

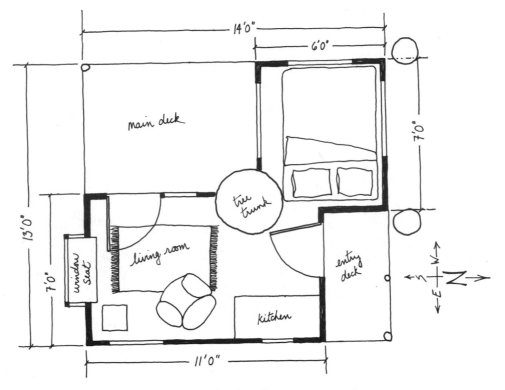

**Figure 32 • Floor Plan for Albert Green's Treehouse**

except where they are cut short by the tree. In retrospect I think it would have been easier to make the short walls the by-walls, because all the short walls contained the roof slopes. Maybe next time.

Before you start to build your frame, you have to decide on the type of siding you want. With ground houses I use plywood for exterior sheathing, but in trees you have to weigh the pros and cons of different materials very carefully. Plywood is very heavy, and that means more work raising it up and more stress on the tree. However, it makes the frame much stronger. Skip sheathing is another option; this is what we used in building Charlie and Henry's treehouse when we nailed 1 × 2s horizontally across the framing at set intervals. I use this only when using shingle siding. It's much lighter but provides less strength.

If you're going with lap-siding, or clapboard, you can attach the siding directly to your studs and opt out of sheathing altogether. If you're building a small treehouse

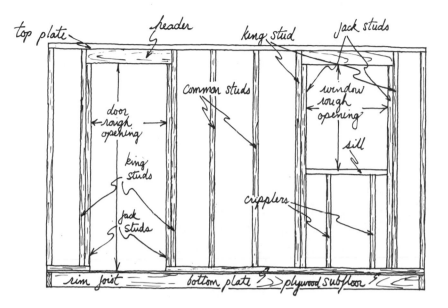

**Figure 33 • The Parts of a Wall**

where the walls are all very short, you can get away with no sheathing, but if you're going for a structure of any size, I recommend sheathing of some kind. Also, if you don't use sheathing you'll have to add extra studs around doors and windows to have something to nail the siding to.

At Albert's we went with ½-inch OSB (Oriented Strand Board) sheathing. It's a kind of plywood. He had a shed full of it so we thought we'd put it to good use and save him some money at the same time. Also, its strength would be appreciated so high off the ground. To save on weight you could go with ⅜-inch plywood, but I don't recommend it with shingles because it doesn't give much for the shingle staples to hold on to.

Plywood has another advantage: since it's already cut square, you can easily square the frame when attaching it—just as you did with the floor up in the tree. Relying on those trusty factory edges, I can frame accurately on the ground and not have to worry about it later when I'm among the branches. Also, you save a ton of time with plywood compared to skip sheathing simply because each sheet covers such a large surface area.

For the wall frames I use one bottom and one top plate. The top plate is

A Vacation Spot in the Air

doubled in standard ground house construction, but one is enough for these small units. The whole frame is made from 2 × 2s nailed together with 12- or 16-penny finish nails. This is plenty strong, and cuts down on weight. The only limiting factor with 2 × 2s is that you can't use thick insulation. But space is a premium up in a tree and the 2 × 2s save cherished inches all around.

Now we are about to get started on the part of the project that goes very quickly and gives real form to your dream. But before you start, familiarize yourself with the basic components of a "stick" wall. Figure 33 shows all of the basic parts.

Find a place on the ground, or set up a table, where you can lay out the largest wall with room to spare. The closer to the treehouse site the better, to cut down on the distance you'll have to haul it when it's ready. Assuming you have a number of straight walls, establish a right angle, with the lower edge as long as the longest wall, and the vertical leg as long as the tallest wall. You can create it by tracing the factory edge of a piece of plywood onto your surface with a pencil. As you build the wall you can check it against this marker to make sure you're keeping things square.

At Albert's house we picked a simple wall to get started. In this case it was the north bedroom wall. Since the idea is to have all the siding, window, and door casing and corner trim in place, it's important to establish some rules to help keep things straight as you move around the house. Primarily, you must keep track of which walls are the by-walls that carry the outside corner detail, and which walls are the butt-walls that have siding all the way to the ends. Inside walls and corners create different circumstances. But let's talk about the outside corners first.

We chose to have the north bedroom wall framed as a by-wall and run the full 7 feet (see Figure 34). This wall will carry the corner trim. The south bedroom wall also has to have the outside corner detail built into it—on the west end only since the other end runs into the tree. The west wall is the butt-wall and does not have corner detailing. On the west wall the shingle siding simply gets cut flush with the outside of the framing.

To follow is a detailed description of the dimensions and construction of the north wall—the wall where we started. If you already understand framing, skim this section.

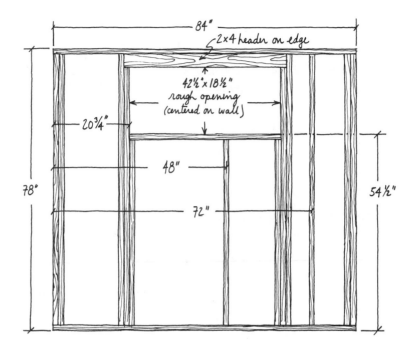

Figure 34 • The North Wall—Wall 1

## The North Wall

The first thing I do when framing a wall is cut the top and bottom plates and mark in full-scale where all of the vertical parts and pieces connect. I mark only one plate to make sure everything lays out properly, then I press the other plate together with the first and transfer my marks across with a speed square. Plans call for a 7-foot-long wall with a window high up in the center. If the window is on hand I double-check its dimensions.

Windows create a secondary set of framing components that include headers, jacks, sills, and cripplers. The header sits above the window and is supported with 2 × 2 jacks sistered against the king studs, which run the full distance from the top plate to the bottom plate. Running horizontally between the jacks at the base of the window is the sill, which is supported by cripplers. Essentially, you're creating two support bridges—one above the window and one below—to support the window frame. I start at the plate by marking the center line of the wall at 42 inches. Since the window itself is 42 inches wide, I designate a rough opening width of 42½ inches.

A Vacation Spot in the Air

I usually allow a ½-inch space on rough framing of windows to make sure they have plenty of room to fit. Nothing is more frustrating than going to set a window up in the tree only to find the frame is too small. Then you'll have to figure out a way to cut the frame wider—and it usually involves a chain saw.

From the center line (at 42 inches), measure back 21¼ inches on either side. These two marks are the inside of the jacks. I put a line across the width of the plate with my speed square, then mark the insides of those lines with the letter "J."

Next mark the inside edge of the king studs, which is 1½ inches farther out. Using the same procedure, I mark these with a "K." To mark the cripplers, measure in 1½ inches from both jacks and label them with a "C."

To mark the remaining common studs and crippler I stick to a 24-inch layout. While 16 inches is more common, with weight a factor, the wider spacing is better. Because most walls are small and windows so plentiful, it's rare you can go uninterrupted using a 24-inch layout, but stick with it so that your plywood sheathing meets up with all of the studs evenly. (Remember that plywood is eight feet long.) To make sure you can easily align the studs when you're ready to nail them down, measure to 24 inches from the edge of the plate, then come back ¾ inch, or half the thickness of the stud. Draw your mark here. That way when you set the edge of the stud on the line, the 24-inch mark lands in the center of the stud. On this particular wall the 24-inch layout adds only one crippler at 64 inches and one common stud at 74 inches. You also need two studs for the ends of the walls. Now all you need to do is establish the height of the header and you can create a final cut list for all of the parts of the wall.

## SETTING THE HEADER HEIGHT

Only the north bedroom wall and the east main room wall are framed at 6 feet 6 inches. All of the other walls have room for header heights of 6 feet 6 inches. In standard construction header heights are set at 6 feet 8 inches but I thought I would save 2 inches. I like to stay consistent around a treehouse with my header height, but since that was not possible on these two walls, I decided the header would be a 2 × 4 on edge that would be tucked directly under the top plate and nailed directly to it. With that established we were able to compile a final cut list for all of the parts of the north wall:

**We took advantage of Albert's flat shop floor to frame walls.**

| | |
|---|---|
| *top and bottom plates* | 84" |
| *7 studs (two of which are kings)* | 75" |
| *3 cripplers* | 51½" |
| *1 header* | 45½" |
| *1 sill* | 42½" |
| *2 jacks* | 71½" |

Armed with your cut list for the entire wall, it's time to break out the saw. The ideal saw for this work is a chop saw, though a standard skill saw will do. A chop saw is nice because it gives good, clean, accurate cuts.

Bring all the pieces over to the floor where your top and bottom plates are waiting and nail everything together. I start with an outside stud and work my way across, sinking two 16-penny finish nails into each stud, top and bottom. Put all the studs in and then go back and nail in the header, putting two nails through each king stud and a few through the top plate down into it. The jacks go in next, sistered up against the kings, nailed every two feet or so. To keep the jacks from twisting I send two nails up through the bottom plate, as I did with the studs. Then I nail the two cripplers into the jacks and set the sill on top of them. I nail the sill down with a nail into the top of each crippler. I'll squeeze that third crippler in after the sill is set. Again, the third one is set "on layout"—in other words, at a 24-inch mark instead of centered between the two other cripplers.

## SHEATHING THE FRAME

The wall frame is now complete. It might not be perfectly square, but the plywood sheathing will quickly solve that problem.

Lay a sheet of plywood on a corner of the frame to square it. I usually start with the bottom plate and lay the plywood horizontally along the base. Line up the end with the end of the wall and nail the plywood with 8-penny box nails every 8 to 10 inches along the bottom plate. Flush up the end of the wall with the 4-foot end of the plywood and nail down that edge. Before putting on the next sheet of plywood, I like to mark any window and door openings directly on the plywood. Then, after nailing it down, I set my circular saw to cut to a $1/2$-inch depth and cut out whatever is marked. I do this as I go because otherwise the openings get covered up and it's a pain to go back and blindly measure and mark their locations. On this north wall, the second sheet required cutting to accommodate the window.

To finish the wall sheathing on the north wall, all that we needed to do was cut the window opening and trim the top 18 inches and end 12 inches of the wall.

## TRIM AND CASING

Once sheathed with all openings cut, I apply the trim. It'd be easy to apply building paper at this point, but I don't often use it. Treehouses aren't going to last forever, and tar paper seems excessive. But use it if you want, especially if you're in a damp climate, or if you're planning on having your treehouse outlive your grandkids.

I start the trimming of the walls with the window. In this case we use $5/4 \times 4$-

inch cedar on three sides and top the window with ⁵⁄₄ × 6-inch cedar. The ⁵⁄₄-inch cedar is roughly 1 inch thick. This thickness will sit flush with the wall shingles, which build up to about an inch, based on a 6-inch exposure. Place the window in the rough opening to make sure it fits. I cut the bottom trim the width of the window, and the sides run from the lower edge of the bottom trim to the top of the window. The top casing runs from the outside edges of the side trim.

Cut all the trim. Set the window against the sill and center it from side to side. Push the trim pieces snug against it and nail them through the sheathing into the frame. It's important to have the casing fit snugly so you won't have to caulk as much later on. It is also important to run a bead of caulk now where the window casing's outside edge meets the wall sheathing. If you are extra concerned about water, you might even install flashing above the top casing.

In most cases new windows come with a thin metal or plastic nailing flange about 1¼ inches wide that protudes from all sides of the window. The flange is nailed through to attach the window to the framing. It keeps the exterior window face an inch or more off the face of the framing, so that siding or casing can be conveniently butted against the window's edge, creating a tight water seal.

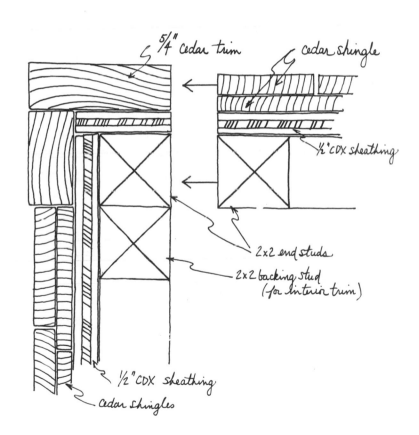

**Figure 35 • Cross Section of a Typical Corner Detail**

A Vacation Spot in the Air

The nailing flange is a convenient and effective feature, but there are a few considerations that need to be weighed before you decide to use them in a treehouse. If you do have an option to use a nailing flange, the decision really lies in whether or not you want to have the windows completely installed before you raise a wall section to its final destination. Using a nailing flange usually eliminates the option of installing windows once the walls are in place, because it inherently creates a task involving dangerous maneuvering high off the ground. If the access is not so difficult then this is not such a problem, and I would recommend that a nailing flange be used.

In my experience it's rare that the nailing flange option ever comes up. It always seems that in treehouse construction I'm using salvaged or left-over windows that don't even have a jamb, let alone a nailing flange. For that reason, treehouse examples in this book describe methods for installing and trimming windows that have no nailing flange.

Next we moved on to the corner trim. This was assembled in roughly the same way as the corner trim for Charlie and Henry's house, but was modified for use with ½-inch plywood sheathing and thicker cedar trim. First I cut a two-inch-wide strip of plywood sheathing the height of the wall. I nailed this to the outside edge of the corner stud of the by-wall so that the sheathing "wrapped" around the frame. When you attach the next wall, which also has sheathing, everything will be flush.

Now break out the table saw and rip two pieces of ¾-inch cedar. Cut one strip of the cedar trim to 2 inches, the other to 3 inches. They run 1 inch above the height of the wall. I tack them on to the corner stud with 10-penny galvanized casing nails (see Figure 35).

The reason the cedar trim runs 1 inch above the height of the wall is because the corner trim has to compensate for the slope of the roof. Most roofs come down across the top of the wall at an angle, so you'll need to cut the top edge of the casing to fit snugly against it. At Albert's treehouse, that angle was 20 degrees.


## SHINGLE SIDING

Now it is time to shingle. Follow the same procedure used in Charlie and Henry's treehouse, including the 6-inch exposure. We used an air compressor and staple gun

**A staple gun makes shingling go faster.**

with 1¼-inch staples to make the job go a little faster. If you don't have access to a staple gun, use 5-penny galvanized siding nails to nail the shingles to the sheathing.

At the top of the wall run your shingles long just as on the kids' treehouse. Don't forget when you cut the shingles to take into account the slope of the roof. This is done so the roof rafters rest on the top plate of the wall rather than on the shingles.

The north bedroom wall is now complete. Follow the plans I've drawn for the remaining seven walls, using exactly the same building techniques we just described. Again, it's important to visualize which walls carry the corner trim so when it's time to fit them together, everything matches up correctly. I worked my way around the treehouse counterclockwise. Following are the diagrams showing all measurements and details.

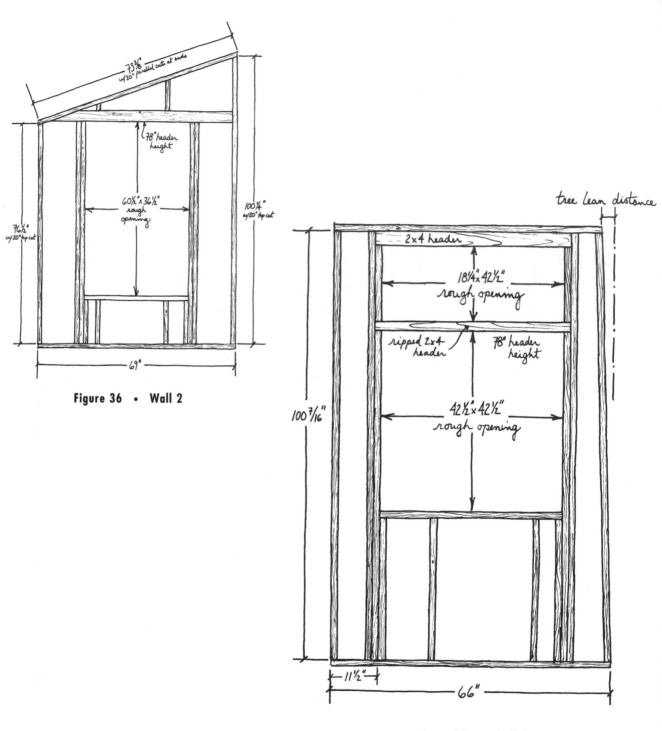

Figure 36 • Wall 2

Figure 37 • Wall 3

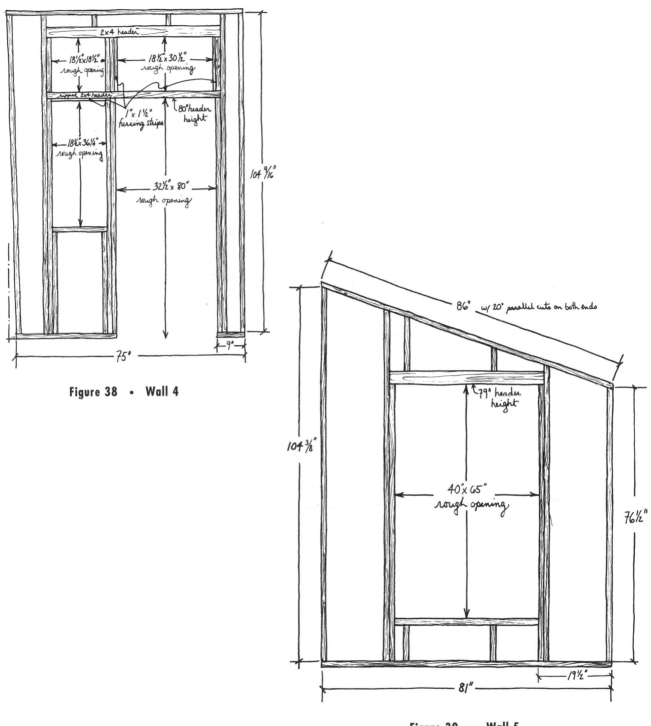

**Figure 38** • **Wall 4**

2x4 header

18½"x18½"
rough opening

18½"x 30½"
rough opening

ripped 2x4 header

1"x 1½"
furring strips

80" header
height

18¼"x 36¼"
rough opening

32½" x 80"
rough opening

104 ⁹⁄₁₆"

75"

9"

86" w/ 20° parallel cuts on both ends

79" header
height

40"x 65"
rough opening

104 ³⁄₈"

76½"

81"

19½"

**Figure 39** • **Wall 5**

97    A Vacation Spot in the Air

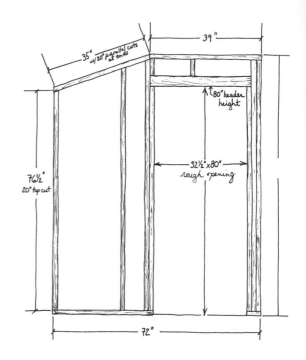

**Figure 41 • Wall 7**

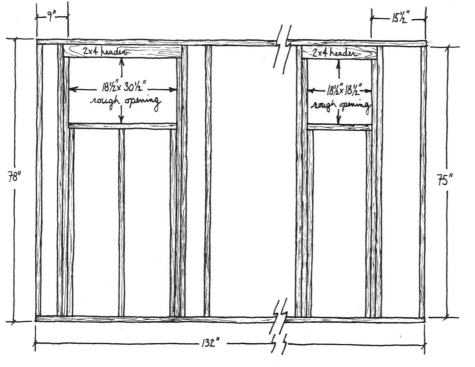

**Figure 40 • Wall 6**

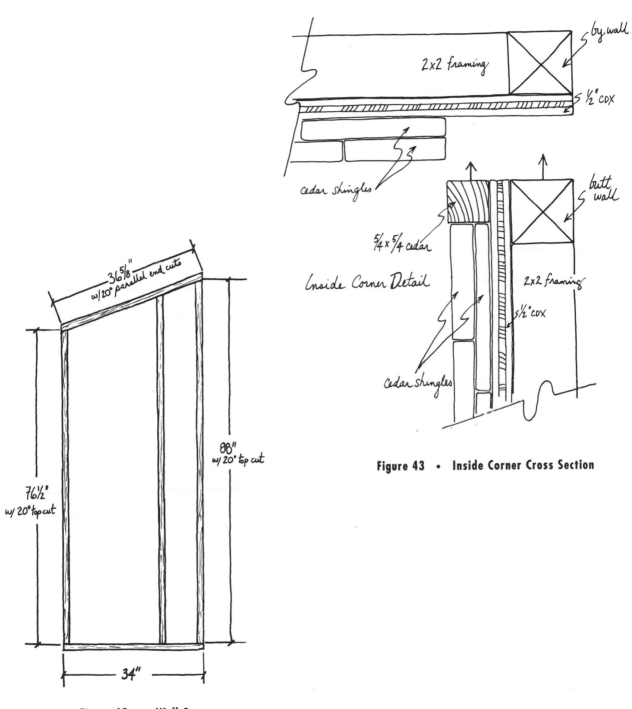

2x2 framing

by wall

½" CDX

cedar shingles

Inside Corner Detail

5/4 x 5/4 cedar

butt wall

2x2 framing

½" CDX

cedar shingles

**Figure 43  •  Inside Corner Cross Section**

36⅝"
w/ 20° parallel end cuts

88"
w/ 20° top cut

76½"
w/ 20° top cut

34"

**Figure 42  •  Wall 8**

A Vacation Spot in the Air

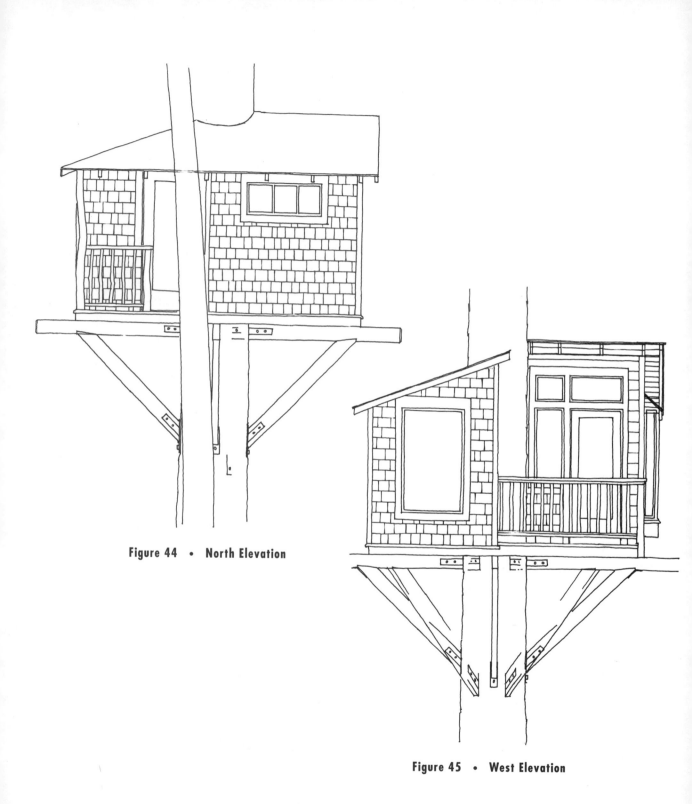

Figure 44  •  North Elevation

Figure 45  •  West Elevation

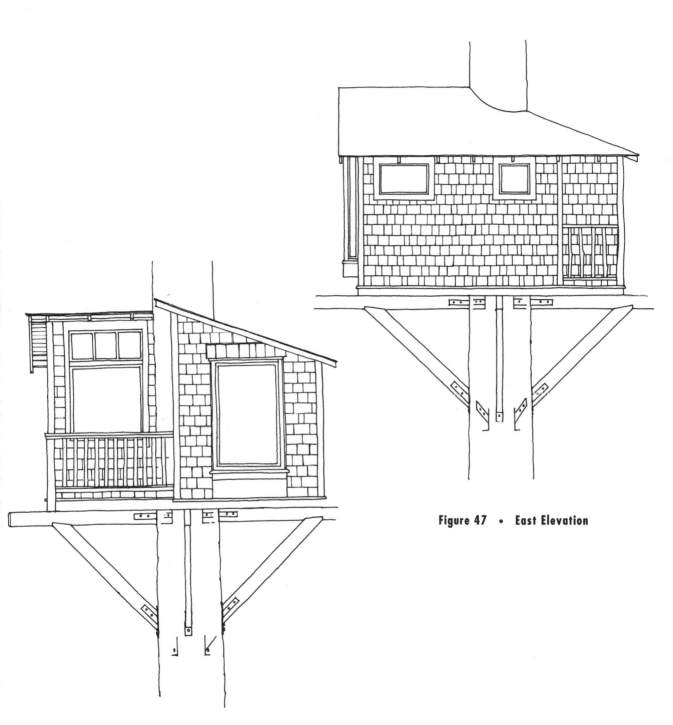

Figure 47 • East Elevation

Figure 46 • South Elevation

## Door Framing

In the west wall of the living room (see Figures 38 and 45), we encountered our first door. I usually use 30-inch-wide doors in my treehouses. This means I must have a rough opening of 32½ inches to accommodate the door jamb, plus ½ inch of room to play. At Albert's treehouse, I cut the door size down to 6 feet 6 inches, two inches shorter than the standard height, so the vertical rough opening was 80 inches, leaving 1 inch for the jamb and another inch above it. You'll need to cut the door itself to accommodate the finished floor. I do that after the floor is in, then cut the door on the ground, where I have more room.

With the fourth wall frame lying on the work surface, and with the plywood nailed down, I ripped the door jamb down to 2¾ inches in depth so it would fit flush with the plywood sheathing on the outside and extend ¾ inch inward beyond the 2 × 2 framing. I extended the frame into the house like this to accommodate the ¾-inch interior paneling that we would install later. Then I cut the door jamb on a table saw to get a clean, straight cut.

I then laid the jamb into the rough opening and screwed it right into the framing on the hinge side—making sure everything was square—using 3-inch screws, one below each hinge. On the other side I left a ½-inch gap, as I did with the windows, to make sure the door wouldn't end up being too big to fit in the frame. To fill that space I stuck cedar shingle shims between the jamb and the rough frame and screwed through the jamb, through the shims, and into the frame. Again, it's important to maintain 90-degree angles at all corners of the door jamb. If you don't, your square door won't fit into the jamb.

## Hoisting the Walls

If you've planned ahead well, when you get to this stage you'll have rounded up a bunch of people to pitch in a hand. This part is fast and fun, and when it's done you'll be able to see the basic treehouse—without a roof, of course.

This is the part of the project where the block and tackle comes in handy—especially if the platform is 30 feet off the ground. Life gets even easier if you have a truck to do the pulling. The double pulley block and tackle I use means that for every

foot I raise a wall, I have to drive six feet. At Albert's that meant a 180-foot drive across his field. If you don't have room for a vehicle, several people will have to suffice.

When lifting a big piece like a wall, tie a second line around it so that as it's being raised someone can "spot" it, or hold it from spinning by keeping the extra line taut as it goes up. The spotter can also guide the piece away from obstructions.

Once the wall is in position on the platform, the bottom plate of the wall will be screwed down to the platform, with the outside of the framing flush with the outside edge of the plywood. However, it would be extremely tricky to line them up by actually looking around the outside of the house, since it's a sheer drop-off, and you'll be busy holding up the wall. So what I do is mark the inside edge of the wall with a chalk line before bringing the walls up. That line should be 1½ inches in from the edge of the platform, which is the width of the bottom plate of the wall. Use that line as your guide for nailing your wall down to the platform.

Bring all your walls close to the hoisting area. You now need to devise a plan for the sequence of wall-raising. We started with the walls farthest from the receiving area (the deck where we planned to receive all the walls) and worked our way in both directions around the house until all that was left were the two walls facing out onto the deck.

Someone on the ground needs to fasten the block and tackle to the wall to be hoisted. Choose a part of the wall frame that has a hole in it to wrap a line around, such as a window or door jamb. Make sure you tie it so it's balanced and so that the top end goes up first, so you won't have to flip the wall around once it's up on the platform. Once the line is tied securely—again, I use a bowline knot, which unties easily after it has been strained—hook the block and tackle around it and have the driver roll off until all slack is taken up and the wall is standing upright on the ground. Then tie the guide line around any part of the frame to keep it from spinning and/or hitting against the tree. If it starts spinning, you'll end up with a fouled block and tackle.

Devise some signals so that the driver of the vehicle knows when to start, stop, and back up. One person works the guide line as the wall goes up. The driver slowly lifts the wall up by driving away from the tree. At least a couple of people are waiting on the platform. With the truck for support it's very easy to swing the wall onto the platform when it reaches the right height.

Unhook the block and tackle when the wall's up and held steady. Line the wall up on your chalk marks and screw it down through the bottom plate using 3-inch self-tapping wood screws set every foot or so. Someone has to brace that wall until the second wall is up and attached to it—if a strong gust of wind came along and no one was there, the wall would probably fall off, since the wood screws in the bottom plate are all that are holding it up.

When the second wall is up, line that one on its mark and butt it snugly against the first wall. Starting at the base of the wall, screw the corner stud of the second wall into the corner stud of the first wall and work your way up. Screw every couple of feet or so using 3-inch self-tapping wood screws. Then screw down the bottom plate. Those first two walls can now stand on their own while you hoist the rest up. When all walls are screwed to the platform and to each other they'll still be a little wobbly. Attaching the roof will fix that, among other things, but before moving on to the roof, let's attach the doors and windows.

**Ian installs windows with finish nail gun.**

## The Doors and Windows

I waited until this point to attach the doors and windows because it made the walls easier to lift, and because I didn't want to worry about breaking glass during the hoisting. You might wait until the roof is framed before you start this phase, but I never have the patience. Set each window into its rough opening so it's resting on the sill. The casing is already on the outside of the wall and should fit around it properly, forming a nice snug frame. Once it's in place, nail it

down with 10-penny finish nails to the frame, or countersink some 2½-inch wood screws.

Now that the windows are in, you need to caulk them where the casing meets the window jamb to seal them against water. Unfortunately, this has to be done from the outside. The safe way to get out there is to lay scaffolding down across your extended beams so you can walk around the outside of the treehouse. (Since you're up in the treehouse, you already have your safety line attached, right?)

Installing the doors is more cumbersome than the windows, but they attach easily. Since your jambs are already in place, all you have to do is haul the doors up and slip them on the hinges. If your jamb is on correctly the door will fit and swing perfectly. If it doesn't—well, I hope you can live with it. Done is better, after all.

## The Roof

With the walls, windows, and doors in place, I move on to the roof. At Albert's house the roof was fairly simple. I built what's called a shed roof. A shed roof works on only one plane and has rafters that span the entire roof. In this case, there were actually two shed roofs, one over the living room area and one over the bedroom area, that met at a 90-degree angle and formed what is called a hip at their intersection.

First you need to know how long your full-spanning rafters are. Starting over Albert's living room space, I climbed up and took a field measurement from the outside edge of the opposite walls, then added 12 inches on both sides for the overhangs. We knew that the roof slope was 20 degrees from our framing of the side walls, so we cut that angle on the ends of these full-spanning rafters just for looks.

I space the common rafters on 2-foot centers and cut as many as I need based on that spacing. I also mark the top plates of both walls, so I know where to screw down the rafters as I'm working my way across. Next I cut the 22½-inch frieze blocks, which fit snugly on top of the top plate between the rafters. Without them there'd be a space between the top of the wall and the roof.

It's best to start from the outside and work your way in. The end rafter sits right on the top plate of the outside wall. I attach it the same way I attach the common rafters—by screwing from underneath through the top plate of the wall frame with 3-inch self-tapping wood screws. Once the end rafter is set, I work my way toward the tree. I cut short the rafters that run into the tree and toenail them directly

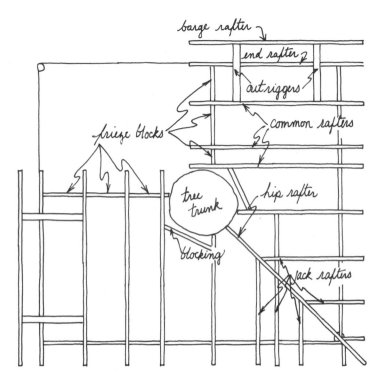

**Figure 48  •  Roof Framing Plan**

into the tree, being sure to maintain the same plane as the other rafters. I do this by extending a 2 × 4 across the top of the rafters I've already set. I hold the shortened rafter snug up against the underside of that 2 × 4 and toenail it to the tree.

I repeated this entire process above the bedroom, going as far as I could until I was ready to install the hip rafter. All along I attached a frieze block after each rafter to ensure a snug fit as I worked my way down the line.

Before I dive into the hip rafter I usually first attach another rafter beyond the two end rafters. This one is called a barge rafter and it basically allows me to have a roof that extends out over the plane of the wall. The problem is that because it runs outside the walls of the treehouse there's nothing to nail it to. Remember, the end rafter is already nailed to the top of the wall. Beyond that is blue sky and, in Albert's case, a 30-foot drop to the ground. So you have to build a series of little bridges that extend perpendicularly from the end rafter far enough out for us to nail the barge rafter into them. These bridges are called outriggers, and are made from pieces of 2 × 4.

To keep them on the same plane as the rafters you have to cut notches in the end rafters 1½ inches deep and 3½ inches wide for the outriggers to pass through. Lay the outriggers flat, with their inside end butted flush up against the first inside rafter and extending through the notch and out another 12 inches (less the 1½ inches for the barge board) beyond the outside rafter.

There are two out-riggers—one of them two feet down from the peak and the other two feet up from the bottom of the roof. To secure the outrig-gers, send two 16-penny galvanized casing nails through that first inside rafter into the end of the outriggers, then sink an-other two down through the face of the outriggers into the notches in the end rafter.

When those are set, attach a barge rafter just as we did on the kids' treehouse. At Albert's it was simply a 2 × 4 with the 20-degree roof slope cut on both ends. Nail it to the two outriggers with two 16-penny galvanized casing nails.

Okay, as I men-

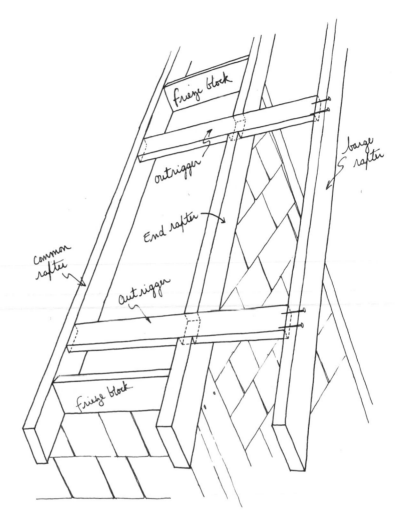

**Figure 49  •  Outrigger Construction Detail**

tioned, you're going to need to set a hip rafter, since this roof has two planes. The hip rafter marks the line where those two planes meet. It runs from the corner of the entry deck on a slope up to the tree. That slope will be slightly less than the slope of the common rafters, since the hip rafter spans a longer distance. Because the length of the hip rafter is shortened by the presence of the tree, you can't use typical rafter layout books to determine its length. So you must climb up and physically measure it. I set up a full-size simulation of the roof planes directly off the existing rafters, just as I did for the common rafters that are toenailed into the tree.

Again, simply extend across a couple of long 2 × 4s, one across from the living room and one from the bedroom rafters. Set them close to the point where the hip rafter will connect to the tree. I tack them down lightly to hold them in place.

Set the hip rafter right up underneath both 2 × 4s, with the lower end resting on the outside corner of the building. Mark a plumb cut on the tree end of the hip rafter, or, if the tree is leaning, scribe a line that matches the tree. Cut this line and temporarily toenail the hip rafter to the tree.

The end of the hip rafter that rests on the corner has to be notched so that it sits at the same plane as the other common rafters. Right now, because the hip rafter slope is less steep, the bottom end is sitting slightly higher than the other rafters. Notch the hip rafter where it sits on the top plate to drop it onto the plane of the common rafters.

I run the hip rafter long, then cut the tail after. On Albert's house, the tail extends beyond the natural wood post on the outside corner of the deck by 17 inches. I go back and nail the hip rafter to the tree and at the seat cut I just made.

Now that the hip rafter's on, you can proceed with the rest of the rafters. Start from where you left off. Rafters that attach to the hip rafter are called jack rafters. They run parallel to the common rafters and are nailed in pairs, with one on each side of the hip rafter. As you approach the corner of the house, the jack rafters get shorter. As with the hip rafter, run them long on the outside so they can be cut accurately once they're installed.

A jack rafter has a compound angle cut into the end where it attaches to the hip rafter. The "school of eyeball construction" teaches us to shoot from the hip on this one. I just hold a piece up in the general position I want and scribe some lines that look good. After a few passes with the skill saw, you should have something that does the job. Use your sample as a model for the remaining jacks.

Remember, the corresponding jack rafter on the other side of the hip rafter is basically a mirror image of the first, so cut both at the same time. Make sure to attach the jack rafters on both sides of the hip rafter as you go, so the hip rafter doesn't bow to one side or the other. Attach them with two toenails directly into the hip rafter.

When they're all attached, you can trim the tails of the jack and hip rafters to match the common rafters. I sink a nail into the end of the outside rafter and hook my chalk line to it. I pull the line across all the way to the hip rafter. I make a 12-inch mark on the jack rafter closest to the hip rafter and make sure the chalk line crosses it. Snap the line and cut it. Then mark a plumb line down the face of each rafter that needs trimming. These are fun cuts to make but be careful; you should hook up a backup safety line for this maneuver.

## Roof Sheathing

We decided to leave the roof rafters exposed on the inside of Albert's house to make it feel more spacious. But Albert still wanted a finished look on the ceiling, so rather than use plywood roof sheathing—which would show underneath—I used $1 \times 6$ tongue-and-groove pine, the same material we later used to finish the interior walls. Albert had also decided not to fully winterize the place, which would have meant insulating the ceiling like the floor, putting the insulation between the rafters and nailing down the tongue and groove on the inside of the rafters.

Rule one on tongue-and-groove roof sheathing is to start from the bottom and work your way up. Have the tongue point toward the peak and set the base of the board flush with the ends of the rafter tails. Use a chalk line to make sure your first course is straight, then secure it with an 8-penny nail into each rafter. Work your way up to the peak, being sure to leave a little overhang at the barge rafter. Let each course run long across the hip rafter.

When you reach the tree, use a jigsaw to cut an appropriate curved end in the boards, leaving about a half inch of space between the roof and the tree. That space will be filled with foam insulation, which can give if the tree grows more. Since the boards are only 6 inches wide, I usually eyeball the curve that needs cutting. You may

**Roof sheeting moves from bottom to roof's peak.**

need to cut it a few times though, so make sure you leave enough overhang off the barge.

At the upper end of the rafters cut the final row of tongue and groove so that it extends about ¾ inch over the edge. If you want to be really precise, rip it at a 20-degree angle so it's plumb.

One roof plane is now complete, with the tongue and groove extending long over the hip rafter. You need to cut this. Snap a chalk line right down the center of the hip rafter. Adjust your skill saw blade to get a perpendicular cut. Also raise your blade a bit so you don't cut into the hip rafter just below the roof boards.

Follow the same steps for the other side. The only difference is you'll have to precut the angle where the boards meet at the hip rafter. Let the boards on the bedroom side run long off the other side of the roof. When they're all nailed down, trim the end to protrude out ¾ inch from the barge board just like the other side.

## The Metal Roof

Albert chose galvanized metal roofing to match his ranch house. I like a metal roof because it's quick and easy to install. It's also hard to beat from a weight standpoint. Since the tongue and groove is so thin, this brings up the issue of how to attach the metal roof to the rafters. If you nail right through the 1 × 6 tongue and groove, the nails will show through.

To avoid this, we laid down 1 × 2-inch sleepers spaced every 18 inches and nailed them through the tongue and groove into the rafters and perpendicular to the rafters.

We were careful to nail into the rafters by following the nail lines on the tongue and groove.

The metal roofing comes in 2-foot-wide strips of various lengths. We used 10-foot lengths that ran from the peak down to the bottom. We were generous with the side overlap between sheets, draping about 6 inches.

I cut all the metal roofing on the ground, using an abrasion blade on my skill saw. It's very important to wear ear plugs and eye protection when cutting metal roofing. Obviously, the sawdust is metal and it tends to fly around just like wood. So make sure other people are far away. Back on the roof, lay down the first 10-foot length so it protrudes about an inch over the side and bottom and top edge of the roof. To get a tight water seal, use aluminum roofing nails with a neoprene washer. Nail into the sleepers every 12 inches. Begin with the next row, overlapping 6 inches. I don't nail down the leading edge of each row, since it's going to be covered by the next length and the aluminum nail heads stick up a bit. After overlapping with the next length, I nail both with one nail.

Just as with the plywood floor, you'll have to scribe around the tree trunk. The pieces that cover the hip rafter need to be cut accordingly, getting that edge as close to the hip rafter's center line as possible. It doesn't have to be exact, because you'll lay a prefab ridge cap over the hip rafter that extends out 4 or 5 inches on either side. Put that on last and nail it into the sleepers.

## Finishing the House

From the outside the house now looks more or less complete. But the inside still needs a finished floor, wall paneling, and door and window casings, and the main deck needs a railing. Beyond that, there are a hundred other details you can add to your home. It's just like interior design in a ground house. It's a process that never ends. I'm going to hit only on the essentials—the things every treehouse needs.

## The Railing

While I was up roofing, Albert was out finding branches to use as balusters for the railings. For obvious reasons we thought a railing fashioned from natural wood would help maintain the ambience of "treedom." Luckily there was a deadfall nearby from which Albert scavenged what he needed. We wanted a simple but strong and safe railing, at least 36 inches high, which is the minimum height under the Uniform Building Code. (The least we could do is comply with that rule!)

Albert cut and skinned all the branches, making sure they were all 30 inches long. He also cut the railing's top and bottom horizontals, which were 2 × 4s ripped down to a width of 2½ inches. So when the roof was done we were ready to start assembling the railing. Laying it out loosely on the ground, we spaced the balusters at 5 inches on center between the top and bottom horizontals. (Balusters should be placed close enough so that a four-inch round ball, approximately the size of an infant's cranium, can't pass between them.) I screwed down into the branches through the top horizontal with two 3-inch screws. The balusters were an average of about 2 inches thick. Then I screwed up from under the bottom horizontal to complete the job.

With all the balusters screwed in, we had our railing segments ready—two for the front deck and two for the entry. The next step was to set the posts. We needed just one for each deck. We had already installed a corner post on the entry deck to support the roof framing. Albert again chose to use pieces of fallen ponderosa with the bark intact to visually tie the railing back to the tree. We toenailed the main deck's corner post directly to the top corner of the deck. The post on the entry deck did not have the advantage of two railings coming into it to make it strong like the one on the main deck, so it needed to be attached differently. I notched the bottom 10 inches so that half of the width of the post rested on the entry deck and the other half extended down and was bolted to the floor joists. I let the horizontals on each railing segment run a little long where the post would go, knowing I'd cut them to size once the irregularly shaped corner post was in. I scribed the ends of the horizontals to get a nice fit with the post. You should be sure to leave a 3-inch space between the deck and the bottom rail. Screw the horizontals into the post from underneath to hide the screw head.

The railing cap adds a nice finishing touch to the railing. It's no more than a simple 2 × 4 laid across and screwed into the top railing from underneath. It has a mitered 45-degree angle where it crosses the corner post.

**A jigsaw is an invaluable tool for scribing.**

### The Floor and Wall Finish

Time to head back inside to complete the floors and walls. To save money on the floor, we did not use standard tongue and groove. Instead, we went with regular 1 × 6 planking. Normally I'd prefer the former, so when the floor shrinks up, as it will, you won't be able to see through the gaps between the boards. At Albert's house it was purely a budgetary decision to go with the plain 1 × 6s.

Cut the boards to size and nail them down to the sleepers, making sure to wedge them tightly together as you go. Again, at the trunk, scribe the boards so they hug the tree smoothly, leaving that ½-inch gap between the floor and tree to allow for tree growth. I use 8-penny ring shank nails. You can also glue the boards down with subfloor glue to reduce squeaking. This floor section should be easy and fast. Before you know it you'll have a finished floor. Congratulations!

## The Walls

You're in the home stretch! At this point your crew usually starts to abandon you. That's okay, though, because you can haul your chop saw and table saw up into the treehouse now and go to town. It's much faster, if you're alone, to cut your wall paneling up in the tree.

**Turn interior paneling vertical for a wainscoting effect.**

This is the part of the job that's the most fun for me. It's like adding the final touches of paint on a painting. The treehouse quickly comes to life as the wood paneling rises higher and higher.

I like to build a wainscoting around the base of all the walls. To do this I turn the tongue and groove vertical for the first 32 inches. (With 8-foot lengths you can get three pieces out of them.) Nailing them on vertically means I have to block between the studs to have something to nail into. I snap a line across the studs at 32

A Vacation Spot in the Air

inches. That mark is the center line for the blocking. For blocking I use whatever scrap 2 × 4 or 2 × 2 is lying around. If you're adding in rigid insulation, you'll want to get a good, consistent, and level line there so you can precut a stack of insulation to fit. If not, just eyeball along your line and toenail into the studs. If you plan for wainscoting from the start, I recommend installing blocking at the wall framing stage. Cut a whole slew of 32-inch tongue-and-groove pieces and prepare for a nailing frenzy. If you held out and didn't use a nailgun, you're going to wish you had one now.

Start at one corner and stick the grooved end right against the corner stud. Nail two nails into the bottom plate and two into the blocking at 32 inches. Don't worry about those nails being exposed. They'll be hidden by a chair rail molding above and the base molding along the floor. Each time you get to a door or window jamb cut the tongue and groove accordingly to make a reasonably snug fit. That seam will also be covered—by the inside casing—so it doesn't have to be exact.

Above the wainscoting I turn the tongue and groove back to horizontal. Set the first row tongue up. Where you can't span an entire wall make sure to cut the first piece to end on the center of a stud so the next piece can share it. Set your corners tight, with one wall's tongue and groove extending all the way to the corner stud and the next wall's tongue and groove butting against the former.

There's only one outside corner inside Albert's house, between the bedroom and the entry. Here we cut a ¾-inch square strip from the same tongue-and-groove material to run the height of the wall. On both sides of that outside corner, we cut the tongue and groove so that each side was flush with the edge of the 2 × 2 corner. The ¾-inch strip fit into the corner, at the ends of the tongue and groove. This way, rather than seeing the exposed ends of the tongue and groove on at least one side, we added a uniform, more finished-looking touch.

When you're nailing down the horizontal tongue and groove, hide the nails by sinking them on roughly a 45-degree angle close to the tongue of the board. You don't need to nail the bottom part of each board, since it's already straddling the tongue from the board below it. With nails along the top, there's no way it'll come free.

## Finishing Touches: Window and Door Trim, Base Molding, and the Chair Rail

There are many styles to choose from when deciding how to trim around your doors and windows. The "picture frame" method uses mitered 45-degree angles at all of the corners and is probably the most common detail used in homes. At Albert's, I cut the door and window casing a little differently; I used a box method, where all of the ends of the trim pieces are square cuts. The top piece, however, extends beyond the side casing by ½ inch on each side and then tapers out to the top on a 10-degree angle.

I used the same tongue-and-groove material for the casing but ripped off the tongue and groove in two separate runs through the table saw and then ripped it in half again to net out with a material width of 2⅜ inches. I used the same 2⅜-inch material to run along the floor as base molding.

To cover the transition from the vertical wainscoting to the horizontal paneling, I fashioned a simple two-piece chair rail. For this I used the same 2⅜-inch flat casing to cover the seam, then ripped a more narrow 1⅛-inch piece and nailed that flat onto the edge of the piece covering the seam.

You are done!

## The Ladder

Oh yeah, the ladder. After nine straight days and about 230 man-hours of labor, I was beginning to grow tired. Despite the beauty of my surroundings I could feel the clouds of indifference sweeping across Pleasant Valley. Soon the treehouse would be cast in their shade. Albert himself seemed to be gripped by ennui. So after a short meeting we were able to rationalize our decision to scrap plans for an elaborate stair system to reach the treehouse. We settled on a removable extension ladder as the way to get up and down.

This worked well for a couple of reasons. First, it was in accordance with our remaining energy level. Second, Albert's treehouse is visible from Pleasant Valley Road. We were both worried that all manner of yahoos burning down that dirt trail would want to stop and climb on up, breaking their necks in the process. Images of drunken teenage couples making love there in deep winter—empty beer cans strewn across the floor—sent one word ricocheting through both our heads, a word that strikes fear in the hearts of all modern Americans: lawsuit.

A retractable ladder would mean Albert could render his treehouse unreachable while he was away. A retractable ladder would mean he could sleep well at night, sure his new home wasn't being vandalized by a truckful of bloodstained redneck poachers staking out the valley with their 30.06's from his lofty perch. Third, I had a retractable ladder with me. I just sold it to Albert on the spot and we were done.

I was happy to have finished Albert's treehouse at last. We'd had a great time and everyone was pleased with the results. Albert invited me to stay on a bit longer, but I had to decline. As much as I loved Montana, I was being called back to Fall City, Washington, to my family, my home. I needed to set foot once again in my trusty office treehouse, to regroup, relax, and map out my next project.

"Albert!" I called as I inched my tippy panel van (a converted Ben & Jerry's delivery truck) onto Pleasant Valley Road. "Call me if you have any questions. Enjoy!"

"Goodbye, Pete!" he called.

In the rearview mirror I could see Albert standing below his treehouse, hat in hand, waving. Then he turned, put one foot on the ladder, and began to climb.

# 6

## Take Your Work to the Sky

**One day a few years ago, when the stars were aligned** just right, my wife, Judy, our three kids, and I went out for a drive about half an hour east of Seattle, into the fertile farmland nestled against the foothills of the Cascade Mountains. That evening, without even looking for it, we stumbled upon the property where we now live. I don't know how we got so lucky, but I'm convinced that the core goodness of treehouses, which had been a part of my life for several years by then, had something to do with it. The parcel of land is five acres of flat pasture with one edge densely forested with large second-growth firs. When we got the chance to walk the property that day, I was drawn straight to the trees and fell into a Swiss Family Robinsonesque fantasy: early morning sunrise; Judy and I making breakfast up in our treehouse cottage; the kids still asleep in their smaller unit just one tree away and connected by a footbridge. This vision would come at least partially true, but I didn't know it at the time.

Judy was just as excited as I was by the site, so we set out to buy the property and move the clan from Seattle. The transaction was fraught with pitfalls, but after eight months we finally acquired the parcel. As quickly as I could, I bought the fam-

---

*Photo at top of page:* **Office work is more fun off the ground**

**Figure 50  •  Fall City Treehouse**

ily a luxury "single-wide" (read: mobile home) with the idea that over time I would convince Judy that family values are easier to teach from a house 12 feet off the ground in a stand of ground firs. Alas, it was not to be. As I began dropping more and more hints, I learned Judy would never consent to moving her young family into a tree. I was crestfallen.

One day, however, I reached the point where I had to do something—even if it was just for myself. I mean, here I was, now the author of a best-selling book on treehouses, and I didn't even own one, much less live in one. I felt like a total fraud, and with each passing day the fear of exposure grew more intense. Fans of the book were writing me letters, asking me about my treehouse. How long had I been living in it? Criminy, I thought. What happens when someone finds out that Pete Nelson, the adventure treehouse builder himself, lives in a mobile home planted squarely on the ground. I grew paranoid, beginning to mistrust my neighbors, even my closest friends. Each night the dream returned:

*I was a Santa-for-hire, working the Christmas season in the lobby of a small New England shopping mall, hosting endless lines of children on my shopworn knee for the minimum wage. Every night, every kid asked for the same thing: a treehouse. And each night when my shift ended I dragged myself across the street to Eileen's, a friendly tavern. There, I'd pull down my synthetic Santa beard and do what I could to deaden the terrible knowledge I carried inside: I was no Santa. Beneath the red suit I was a fraudulent wish-granter, a man with no powers whatsoever to make kids' treehouse dreams come true. Once upon a time I'd written about other people's treehouses, but that was many years ago . . .*

*Then, one night a passing child appeared in the window. I recognized him from the mall that evening. Of course, he'd asked me for a treehouse, just like all the other kids. I'd probably promised 500 treehouses that day alone when this little guy got to me. He had huge blue eyes and a sad smile.*

*"A treehouse?!" I'd said to him in my best Santa voice. "Sure, why not? I can whip you up a treehouse, no problem! In fact," I continued, "I live in a treehouse at the North Pole!"*

*The boy in the window was holding the hand of his mother and pointing, smiling. "Mom," he cried, "look!" Then, after he'd gotten a closer look at my pathetic state, at my swollen eyes and bulbous red nose, his expression turned to bewilderment. Finally I couldn't take it anymore. "Get outta here, kid! Beat it, I tell ya!" I screamed. But he wouldn't leave. He just pressed his pink little face against the window and began to cry, over and over, "Mom, what happened to Santa? I'm never gonna get my treehouse, treehouse, treehouse, treehouse . . ."*

And each night I'd wake up in a cold sweat, feeling lower than ever. I knew I couldn't begin my second book until I was a treehouse-owning guy like all the people I'd written about the first time around. That's when I got my idea.

## World Treehouse Organization Headquarters

I'd put my office in a tree, by golly. It was the perfect compromise between ground and sky, family and work. I headed out to my stand of firs to find that "right" tree.

In recent years I've become more and more interested in working with reclaimed materials, from wood to windows to doors to whatever supplies I need to complete a treehouse. Using salvaged products is a natural idea, and I've become friends with a salvage specialist who makes this very easy. I've always loved lumber yards, but my friend Jake's yard in Tacoma (Resource Woodworks, Inc.) has become my favorite of all. He shares 10 acres with an 91-year-old sawyer, and when I walk through the stacks of rough-cut cedar and salvaged beams and lumber from demolished buildings I start to salivate. Recycled materials are more and more in demand,

**Ninety per cent of the materials that went into this treehouse were salvaged or left over from other projects.**

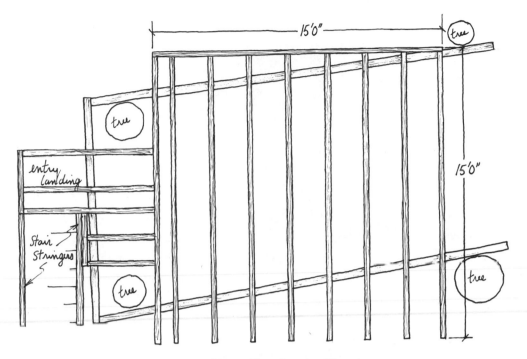

**Figure 51  •  Floor Framing Plan**

which has driven the prices up over the last few years, but it's still a better deal than buying new, especially on dimensional lumber.

Jake let me cruise around the yard and pick out beams for the office treehouse foundation. I found eight perfect 18-foot 3 × 13-inch old-growth fir timbers for joists that had come from an old warehouse in Portland, Oregon. I also bought two 20-foot 6 × 12s for my beams. Happy as a clam, I had that delivered to the site.

This project had to be done cheaply and easily, since it was coming out of my own pocket. This should be a good example of how to really crank one of these out.

I went with a fixed multiple-tree foundation because I had a perfect stand of trees. The design is modeled after the small cottages found in any of the old neighborhoods of Seattle. Even before I had my plans finished, the lumber I'd ordered from Jake arrived. I began working right away. In the end it took about 350 man-hours to complete.

I built between four trees, using two main beams and eight joists. Because I am not actually too big on heights, I decided to set this one just ten feet off the ground. It also meant I could go with a rigid, fixed-frame foundation, as it appeared

**Raising the first beam for WTO headquarters.**

there would be little tree movement, especially since all four would be connected together. It was also much easier lifting materials that short distance. Building at a low height taught me another great lesson. I learned that you don't have to be a mile up in a tree to capture that sensation of being off the ground. In fact, even at six feet you feel as if you've escaped ground life.

The lie of the two main beams depends entirely on the spacing of the four trees they attach to. In my office you can see that the beams are hardly parallel. But it doesn't matter; the squaring comes when you build your floor frame and "roll" your floor joists into position. All you need to do now is make sure your platform is the proper size for the treehouse you're building, and level.

To start I pulled a tape between the trees to measure the length of my beams. (You should cut the beams so you have a foot or two of overhang.) I used a pulley to lift one end of the beam up to a spot on the tree that looked like a good starting point, then predrilled for a $3/4 \times 10$-inch galvanized steel bolt. After sinking that, I hoisted the other end and adjusted it until it was level. I pulled a string across and used a string level to find the point on the other tree from which to start the same process of hanging the other beam.

With the beams up and level, the next step was to "roll" the floor joists. My treehouse is $15 \times 15$ feet, but I cut all eight of the floor joists to 14 feet 9 inches to compensate for the thickness of the one and only rim joist at the back of the house.

The rim joist is 15 feet. I marked the rim joist on 24-inch centers where the common joists would attach.

When building a treehouse like this one, the first thing I do is haul all of the common joists up and lay them on their sides across the beams. Now I have some scaffolding to walk on as I square up my rim and end joists. But in the case of my office, before hoisting the common joists I wanted somehow to acknowledge the beautiful material I was working with. I decided to cut a decorative end on the joists on the front of the house where they're cantilevered. I created a pattern and cut it with a jigsaw, repeating it on all eight joists. This gives the house a look like the stern of an old sailing ship—an object a treehouse resembles in many ways.

Once all the joists are on the platform, I roll the two end joists so they're 15 feet apart on their outside edges. If you're following this design, don't nail them to the beams yet. They'll stay right where they are. Hoist the rim joist up against the backs of the end joists using a pulley on both ends. Nail it, using four pole barn nails (these are 8 inches long) into the backs of the end joists. Now you've got a U-shaped frame, 15 feet on all three sides, which needs to be squared up before being nailed to the beams. The easiest way to ensure you've got the platform frame squared is to use the old "X check," but rather than waiting to have all of the joists attached, do the X check now before it gets too heavy to adjust. First,

**Rolling the floor joists into place.**

nail a temporary board at the open end of the end joist to create a closed box with four sides measuring exactly 15 feet. Measure the hypotenuse from the far end of one of the end joists to the far end of the rim joist. Now measure the hypotenuse running in the opposite direction. Adjust the end joists until those distances are equal. Once you're all squared up, toenail the end joists where they cross the beams.

Now roll the remaining six joists and set them on the 24-inch marks on the rim joist. Nail through the rim joist as you did with the end joists, using three pole barn nails. Now you can go to the other end and knock the joists into line before toe-nailing them to the beams.

I blocked the front end of the joists with pieces of 2 × 6, to add support for the plywood floor. It also served to block the end of the cavity for the R-19 insulation. Since this is a year-round structure, I wanted to insulate it on all sides. The R-19 comes in 22½-inch batts, which fit tightly between the joists on the underside. Before attaching it I laid down the plywood floor on top of the joists, just as I did at Albert's house in Montana. This floor, at 15 × 15 feet, was even easier. Remember to align your tongue-and-groove edge so it's perpendicular to the joist, to take advantage of the support it offers.

Once the floor's on, you can insulate it. I measured down 5½ inches on both sides of the floor joists and snapped lines across them (this is easier to do on the ground before the joists are up in the tree, I learned). I sistered 1 × 2-inch furring strips along those lines—so I would have something to nail the plywood covering to once I finished insulating—and then stuck up the insulation. Then I ripped ⅜-inch plywood (T-111) down to 21¼-inch pieces to seal up the insulation. I nailed the plywood into the 1 × 2 furring. The T-111 has a nice side to it, often used for soffits. I made sure that side faced down.


## The Walls

The platform ready, I headed back to my nearby open-air shop to construct the walls. I went with skip sheathing as opposed to plywood because I happened to have a bunch of 1 × 2s lying around. The skip sheathing is great because it's lighter, and I wasn't concerned about the wind since I was building so low.

## SHEATHING AND FLASHING

I apply the same framing principles to these walls as I did at Albert's and the kids' treehouses. But instead of tacking on plywood to my 2 × 2-inch framing, I applied skip sheathing every 6 inches horizontally up the height of the wall, beginning flush against the bottom plate. Door and windows are also framed the same way as Albert's, cutting the skip sheathing flush with the rough openings.

What we are really doing is combining certain aspects of Albert's wall framing method with certain aspects of the kids' treehouse wall framing method. The overall technique is still the same, but a few adjustments need to be made to have the walls come together perfectly in the tree.

First of all, because of the larger size of the structure, and the fact that I wanted it insulated, I framed all of the walls with 2 × 2s. The skip sheathing was applied on top of the framing, unlike the kids' treehouse, but in the same way we applied the OSB sheathing at Albert's. If you plan on framing this

**Apply window casing before shingling, while wall is still on worktable.**

way, it would be helpful to imagine the skip sheathing as plywood sheathing, only ³/₄ inches thick. This thicker dimension will be important when considering corner trim details and wall lengths for inside corner walls.

Second, as with the shingle siding on the kids' treehouse, there needs to be flashing applied behind the connections of the window and door casings where they butt up to shingles. This is not necessarily a perfect solution to a potential water problem, but I have found it works well in my neck of the woods. Besides, we are building treehouses here, not submersibles.

Shingling is a family affair.

Long walls are split in two to keep them lighter and more manageable. We filled in shingles where the walls met after they were connected. Later we added a window on this east face.

## The Roof

My office has a pyramid-shaped roof and uses 2 × 6-inch rafters. It has four hips. The peak is 48 inches above the top plate of the walls and the overhang extends 16 inches all around. As with Albert's house, the roof involves compound angles. (Aren't you all recent graduates of the school of eyeball construction?)

Begin by measuring and cutting the four common rafters. Each one runs from the center point of each side to the peak of the roof. To measure that length, make a full-size layout using one sheet of plywood. Lay a sheet of 4 × 8-foot plywood on the ground. One corner represents the 48-inch high peak of the roof. Measure out 7½ feet (90 inches) from the corner below that one and mark it. That mark represents the outside edge of the top plate of the wall and is actually where your common rafters cross the outside edge of the treehouse. Now that you have these points marked, place a straight 10-foot-long 2 × 6 rafter down on the plywood template so the top of the 2 × 6 touches the roof peak mark and the bottom of the 2 × 6 touches the 92-inch base line mark along the bottom of the plywood. For the end that rests on the top plate of the wall, cut what is called a "bird's mouth," which allows the rafter to sit squarely on the top plate of the walls. Also trim the rafter tail—the part that sticks out beyond the wall and creates the overhang—down to 3½ inches. To me this smaller rafter tail seems nicer than the 5½-inch depth of a 2 × 6 given the small scale of the treehouse.

### CUTTING AND SETTING THE COMMON RAFTERS

The easiest way to make this bird's mouth cut is to simply drop the entire roof by the distance needed to turn your rafter tails from 5½ inches deep to 3½ inches deep. First, trace the bottom line of your rafter, then mark a parallel line 2 inches in from that. This new line will give you the bottom edge line for the finished rafter. Now bring the rafter from its first position down to this second position and continue the base line created by the base of the plywood template by marking the face of the rafter. Draw another line 3½ inches down from and parallel to the top edge of the rafter. Carry that line from the point that it intersects with the base line to a point 16 inches away

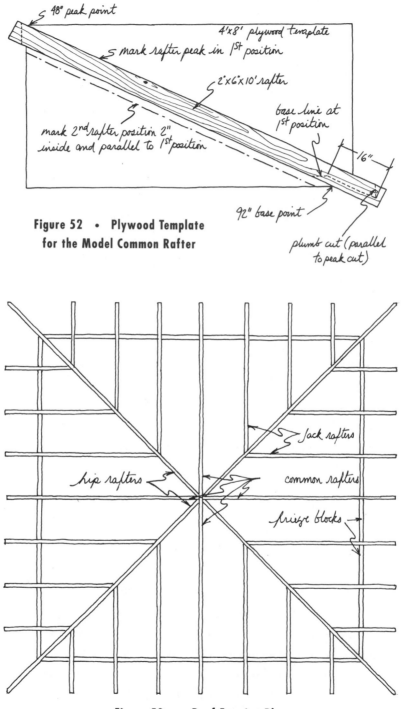

48" peak point

4'x8' plywood template

mark rafter peak in 1st position

2"x6'x10' rafter

base line at 1st position

16"

mark 2nd rafter position 2" inside and parallel to 1st position

92" base point

plumb cut (parallel to peak cut)

**Figure 52 • Plywood Template for the Model Common Rafter**

jack rafters

hip rafters

common rafters

frieze blocks

**Figure 53 • Roof Framing Plan**

from the peak. Now mark two parallel lines, one created where the rafter crosses the 4-foot edge of the template and the other at the 16-inch overhang point.

Once those are cut, trim two rafters an additional ¾ inch each at the peak cut, to compensate for the opposing rafters that abut each other in the four-way peak connection.

Enough with models. Now it is time to try and piece this pyramid roof together. This is a two-person job and I recommend using scaffolding to reach the peak of the roof easily. Before you get set up on your scaffolding, go around and mark the center line of each of the four sides. Pull to one side or the other by ¾ inch and mark a straight line with your speed square and an "X" on the appropriate side. These will be the points you shoot for when erecting these first rafters.

Set up two opposing common rafters on their marks. Send a 2 × 6 ceiling joist all the way across the center line of the house, from one top plate to the other, to tie the ends of the rafters together. You will need some 2 × 4 temporary bracing to keep things from toppling over. Nail through the joist into the rafters, and toenail the rafters and the joist to the top plate at your marks. (Again, this is a two-person job.) Toenail the two rafters together at the top.

Set up the other two commons that you have already trimmed ¾ inch from the peak and toenail them into the top plate and into the other two rafters at the peak.

## CUTTING AND SETTING THE HIP RAFTERS AND JACKS

Time for the hip rafters. They're longer and therefore hang at less of an angle than the common rafters. This means your bird's mouth needs to be cut a little deeper. Where the hip rafters meet at the peak you've got to cut a point for them to fit against the common rafters. This is another compound cut. I usually have to make a few passes at this one with my skill saw to get a good fit. Leave the rafter long so you have room for this type of adjustment. Back on the tail end, adjust the bird's mouth cut so you have the same depth where the rafter passes to the outside of the house as in the common rafters. The overhang for this piece will be close to 22 inches. I keep it long and then come back and give it a plumb cut once all the other rafters are in. Once one hip rafter is cut you can base the other three on it. At the peak I toenail

🌳 Take Your Work to the Sky

**As roof goes on, thoughts turn toward entry design.**

the hip rafters from the top. I also toenail the bird's mouths to the top plate of the wall.

There are three 2 × 6 jacks running between the common and hip rafters. Measure the distance from the tail end of one hip rafter to a common rafter. Divide this by four to get even spacing for the jacks. When cutting the jacks you've got a compound angle to deal with. Again, do the math if you want or use the patented Pete Nelson short-attention-span-for-trigonometry method, eyeballing it and making cuts until you get it more or less right. I use that cut as a template for the remaining jacks. One of the reasons I'm not doing back flips to get all of my joints perfect on the roof framing is because I'm laying down a flat ceiling that will hide everything above.

Sister 15-foot ceiling joists to each jack. The ceiling rafters run across the house from top plate to top plate in just one direction. I lay the interior paneling directly up against those rafters—in this case, 6-inch shiplap, the precursor to plywood (more on this later). Once your ceiling joists are in, go back and install your frieze blocks.

## THE ROOFING

In Seattle there's always a race to get the roof on before it rains, so I kept my attention focused upward. That meant cutting and nailing down the plywood roof sheathing. I had a bunch of leftover OSB ½ inch plywood from a previous job so I used that. In a way, I felt I was recycling.

I decided to use 3 tab asphalt composition roofing, which is very easy to install, albeit a little heavier than I'd like. Cedar shingle would be ideal, since it's so much lighter. But budget constraints and a desire to clean out a growing pile of stored materials pushed me to go with the composition. The simple, pyramid shape of the roof made things even easier.

**Roof rafters are in place and ready for sheathing.**

As with shingles, you *must* lay an undercourse, or first layer, on the low edge of the roof. Be sure with the next course to split the tabs, staggering them as you work your way to the peak. Cut the composition with a utility knife along the center line hip rafter. The final step will be to lay a ridge cap over the hip rafters. I make the ridge cap by cutting single segments from the 3-tab composition. I start at the low edge of the roof and overlap my way to the peak, just as I did on the broad surfaces of the roof. At the peak, trim the composition so it fits snugly together. Let one single segment of composition from a hip rafter extend over the peak to form a cap.

Wiring goes in before insulation and interior finish work starts. I recommend brushing up on basic wiring before you begin.

## Wiring

Now I turn my attention back to the interior. My office treehouse, unlike Albert's pleasure domicile, has electricity. Bottom line is, I can't work in the dark. So, before we can hang interior insulation and paneling we've got to put the electrical system in.

Wiring is a tricky business. I highly recommend heading down to the local hardware store and picking up a book on the basics. Some things need to be planned out in advance: Where do you want sockets? Where will your lighting go? What about phone jacks? Depending on how high-tech you want to be, you might need a few 15-amp circuits. In my treehouse I decided to put the lights and outlets on one circuit and have a dedicated circuit just for the floor heaters. But this has created a huge problem for me; I can't listen to my Mariners' games with the lights on because the radio hums. So figure out the best way for your interests and needs.

We're not electricians, but wiring a treehouse is really pretty easy. Once you've grasped the basic concepts, it won't take you long to wire something on your own. As you're wiring your place, it's a good idea to use metal nail plates on the studs through which live lines pass, to eliminate the risk of sinking a nail into your power as you're putting up your paneling. The nail plates are 1½ inches wide and fit perfectly to the studs with nails that come with them. Depending on the lighting you choose, you'll also have to set your light wells. I have eight recessed lights in my ceiling. I found them very easy to install.

If you build your treehouse in a remote location you might look into alternative energy sources, like solar or wind power. In the last few years there have been some big advances in this area and there are now many retailers selling all kinds of convenient and reliable power systems. I list the address of The Real Goods Company as a good source of information in the resources section at the end of the book.

My treehouse is almost 400 feet from my house. At first I had grand plans for a properly sized underground cable that would come up into a subpanel with its own circuit breakers and code-meeting accoutrements. As a temporary measure I ran a standard ten-gauge house wire right across the ground to the house and plugged it into a 20-amp circuit. That's how it's been since and I'm just fine with it.

Once you've wired the place and have tested everything, put up your shiplap ceiling. Shiplap consists of flat 1 × 6-inch boards with the edges cut to overlap with each other. Tack the shiplap up with 2-inch finish nails shot through a finish gun. When you reach the light wells, scribe around them and continue on until the ceiling is complete. I cut an access panel in the ceiling so I can get up to insulate the small attic space. When the shiplap paneling was all on, I climbed up and rolled out R-19 insulation between the ceiling joists.

**Fit 1½-inch rigid foam insulation between exterior and interior paneling.**

## Paneling the Walls

Cut rigid 1½-inch insulation to fit between the wall studs. It pops in easily and stays up because it's stiff. Now panel the walls with more shiplap. Follow the standard wainscoting and paneling procedure used at Albert's treehouse.

I fashioned the window casing from standard house trim that has a slightly fancier profile than the stuff used on the other treehouses. I picture-framed the casing. Next I hung the doors. Then I put up my railing.

Windows nearing completion.

Ian marks the "reveal" on the windows before installing the casing.

## Finishing Touches

Knowing that I was going to be spending a lot of time in the World Treehouse Organization headquarters, I wanted to do a really nice job on the interior. I decided to lay down a strip floor of fir I rummaged from some old building. For the paneling, I created a white wash by thinning out latex paint. I used the trim color I'd chosen for the outside and thinned that out to use on the wainscoting.

Since moving my work aboveground, business has been steady and rewarding. It may just be a coincidence but sometimes I feel as if something mysterious and wonderful came together after I finished my office. I gained new perspective and sensitivity both for trees and for my work in them. Now if I could just convince my family to make the big move skyward . . .

Railing designs can vary widely. I chose to go with tight spacing between ballasters for a more substantial look.

Completed railing. For scale I dropped the height of the top rail to 30 inches from floor. Standard height in a house is at least 36 inches.

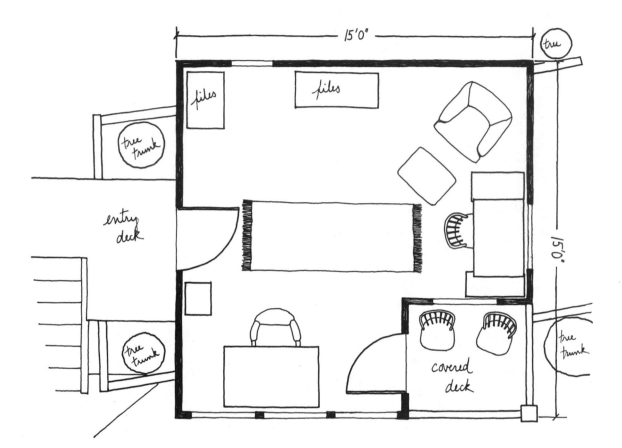

15'0"

tree

files

files

tree trunk

entry deck

tree trunk

15'0"

tree trunk

covered deck

**Figure 54 • Floor Plan for
Fall City Treehouse**

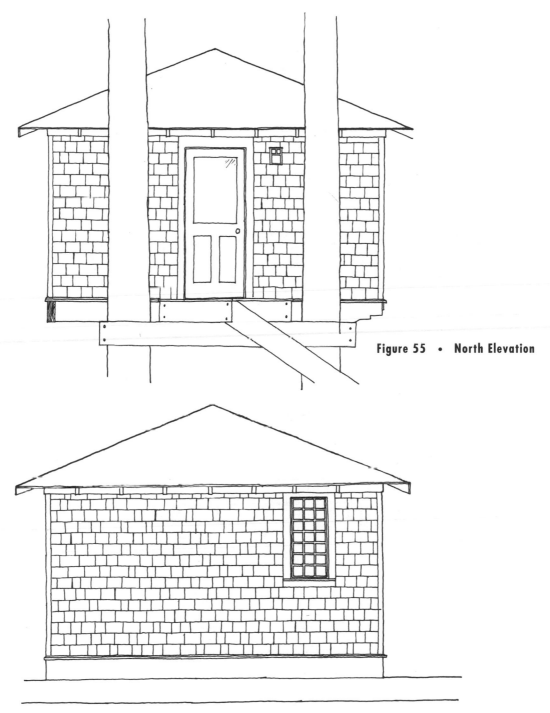

**Figure 55** • **North Elevation**

**Figure 56** • **East Elevation**

Take Your Work to the Sky

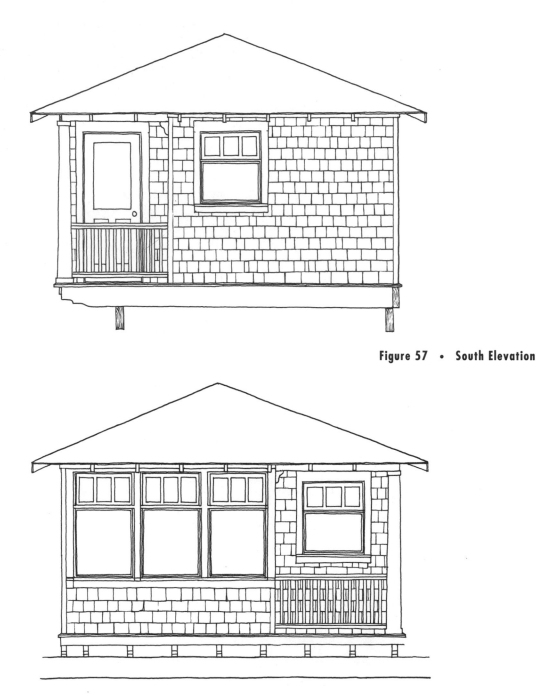

Figure 57   •   South Elevation

Figure 58   •   West Elevation

# 7

## Revisiting Gus's House

**Remember Gus, our dog-mushing, summer-fishing, scraggly** bearded young friend on the Kenai Peninsula in Alaska? Here's how we built his treehouse.

In the true spirit of treehouse construction, budget was the overriding concern here. Scrounging for building materials has long been one of my favorite activities and since treehouses use so much recycled stuff, I believe it is one of the reasons they are so dear to my heart. When I arrived in Alaska to build with Gus, I knew it would be a challenge to find all our supplies, so I went with an open mind and a willingness to experiment with new building materials.

Our first stop in Anchorage was Spenard's, the local building supply store. I was relieved to see that prices were not too far out of line from what I was used to in Seattle. They were still high enough to send Gus into a mild depression, but he kept his chin up and we managed to fill our friend John Bramante's pickup truck for our three-hour journey to the Kenai Peninsula.

As a big baseball fan, I am somewhat superstitious, so every time I approach a new project I am on the lookout for positive and negative signs. In the past bad

*Photo at top of page:* **Gus securing one of the first bolts in the foundation of his arboreal palace.**

omens have come in the form of a vanishing tape measure or the sudden appearance of a dead coyote on a building site. The good omens I look for include nearby living wildlife, such as Orca whales or eagles. This time I was excited and relieved on our drive to Clam Gulch to spot a small pod of Beluga whales on a parallel course just off the highway in Turnagain Arm Bay. Signs like these always relieve any perceived pressures that I tend to conjure up. I began the project in good spirits.

## The Foundation

Gus's newfound property is a flat, three-acre stretch of spruce platted out of a forest that stretches across the entirety of the Kenai Peninsula. It is ideal for his mushing lifestyle, as he can hook up his dogs and vanish through his backyard into a Jack London wonderland.

My only reservations about the site were the clear indications of recent bear visits nearly everywhere we stepped. While Gus had done a fine job of settling the front of the property by the road, the back of the property is pure Alaska wilderness, scat and all.

A nice feature of Gus's land is its density of mature spruce trees. The trees on the Kenai Peninsula do not grow tall, maybe sixty feet at best, but all of Gus's are in good health. A BeetleKill in the area has everyone a little concerned about the long-term viability of the trees, and Gus was told to avoid the oldest trees as they appeared to be the most susceptible to the beetles. We found a well-located grove of spruce that appeared to be in its prime.

After our traditional "tree blessing," we fired up the Husky (Gus's Huskquevarna chain saw) and went in search of the treehouse beams. We used tree trunks themselves for the beams. We had to say a few more blessings that afternoon. We cut the first tree to span the 19 feet from tree B to tree C. I added four feet to the length to compensate for the thickness of the trees (approximately 12 inches) and to give it a one-foot overhang on each end. Naturally, we had chosen to go with the fastest, least expensive method of attachment. With a rigid fixed-frame foundation we wanted to keep the house as low as possible. We bolted the first beam approximately 6 feet off the ground with ¾-inch galvanized lag bolts that extended 6 inches into the support tree. Since we were working directly off the ground, this process went very quickly. With four helpers we had all four beams up and three support

**Figure 59  •  West Elevation**

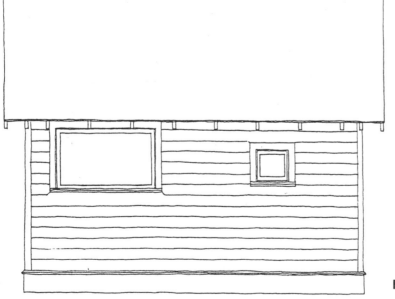

**Figure 60  •  North Elevation**

Revisiting Gus's House

Figure 61 • East Elevation

Figure 62 • South Elevation

posts set midway along the three longest spans by the end of one long afternoon.

Since Gus's treehouse was close to the ground we chose to make the three posts rigid. We did this by carving out a rounded saddle on the top of the post with a chain saw. The beam rests in this "pocket." We then nailed the post into the beam from below with long spikes. At the base I like to use preformed concrete pier blocks that have a metal saddle formed into

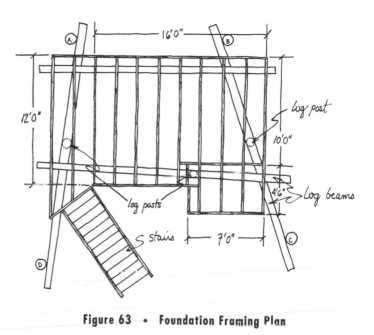

**Figure 63 • Foundation Framing Plan**

them. I bury the concrete so just a few inches protrude from the soil. The metal saddle keeps the post from coming in contact with the ground. Because the saddle is made for a 4 × 4 to fit into it, I use a chain saw or a skill saw to cut in two slots so the round post fits in the saddle. I then drill a hole through the post to line up with the holes preset in the saddle, and use a ½-inch carriage bolt to secure the post to its base.

I have noticed that rigid posts are not ideal in treehouses that need a lot of play or are fixed high up in a tree. In this case I use a sliding post for midspan support. Fabricating a 4-inch sliding steel post is obviously more expensive, but it allows a great deal more flexibility. It is also important to make sure your soil will support a preformed pier. It may be necessary to dig down to better soil and pour in a few bags of concrete.

One thing I highly recommend but that we did not do on Gus's house is to strip the bark from the posts and beams before building. A draw knife is a good tool for this. I have also seen adzelike blades mounted to the ends of poles to allow stripping from a standing position. At any rate, this is an important step that will help preserve the life of the logs. Keeping the bark on tends to trap in moisture. The bark is also a good home for insects and disease, which leads to rot. Gus plans to strip them in place when he gets the time. (With all those dogs to tend, I better not hold my breath.)

With all the beams in place, the next order of business was to lay down the floor joists and get the floor done. Gus had bartered some of his trees for a nice pile of rough-cut lumber large enough to frame his entire project plus

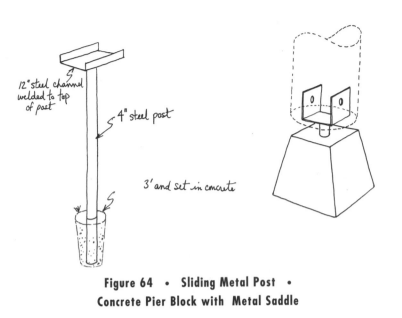

**Figure 64** • **Sliding Metal Post** • **Concrete Pier Block with Metal Saddle**

a few dog houses. I used my electric power planer to take down the humps and knots in the cross beams so the floor joists would all lie flat. As in my office treehouse, the procedure was simple.

With two people, we had the floor framed and the plywood floor nailed off in just half a day. We temporarily nailed down plywood over the deck area until we could come back and put on cedar decking.

## Wall Framing

**O**n Gus's house we framed the walls a little differently than we did on the other houses in the book. The main difference: We went with 2 × 4s instead of lighter 2 × 2s. This was because we wanted to put in thicker insulation, given that Gus lives in Alaska. The other big difference was that we framed the walls directly on the treehouse floor. All the green lumber made the walls very heavy, so rather than building them on the ground and hauling them up, we decided to frame them on the platform itself.

As we sat scratching our heads, figuring out which wall to start with, another crew insulated between the 2 × 10-inch floor joists from below with R-30 fiberglass. We covered all insulation with 4-millimeter-thick plastic to temporarily keep out vermin. Gus has since gone back and put up more durable ⅜-inch plywood.

Meanwhile, our heads were really beginning to hurt from all the scratching, so we decided just to start with the entry wall, a gable end wall, and work our way clockwise around the house.

## Laying Out and Building the Gable End Wall

To measure, cut, and frame the walls, I drew full-size layouts right on my work surface. This helps take the mystery out of measurements and angles. Having a nice, clean plywood floor (presumably square and true) gave us a perfect surface to make our layout simple and accurate.

This method makes drawing a framing layout directly on the floor particularly simple because we were able to use the 12-foot edge as our plate line and the 16-foot edges as our wall lines. We had only to establish our wall heights and roof pitch to complete the perimeter marks of our layout.

We set the wall height at 7 feet 6 inches and decided to use a 10-in-12-foot roof pitch. We also decided to make the two end walls by-walls: They run by the butt-walls and carry the trim detail. This should sound familiar; basically, we were building a larger version of Charlie and Henry's gable end walls. Here is how to lay this out:

Mark the wall heights at 7 feet 6 inches along the 16-foot edge of the floor. Snap a chalk line between the wall height marks. This should create a squared box of 7 feet 6 inches × 12 feet. I like to check the squareness of this by taking an "X-check." Measurements should be the same. If they are not, your box is not square.

Pull your tape along the 12-foot top and bottom lines and find their midpoint (in this case, at 6 feet). Snap a vertical line from these two midpoints that extends above the top line by 6 or 8 feet. This is your center line. Your roof peak will lie somewhere along it.

To find the exact peak point, I take the pitch—in our case 10-in-12 feet—and apply it directly to the full-scale layout on the platform. This was particularly easy here because our 6-foot center line made a 10-in-12 ratio easily convertible to our

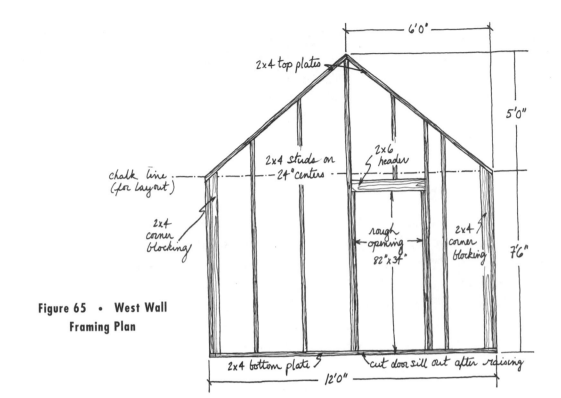

**Figure 65 • West Wall Framing Plan**

2x4 top plates

6'0"

5'0"

2x4 studs on 24" centers

2x6 header

chalk line (for layout)

2x4 corner blocking

rough opening 82"x34"

2x4 corner blocking

7'6"

2x4 bottom plate

cut door sill out after raising

12'0"

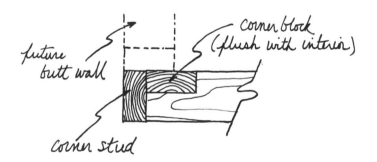

future butt wall

corner block (flush with interior)

corner stud

**Figure 66 • Corner Block Detail for 2 x 4 Framing**

full-scale dimensions. A 10-in-12 pitch is the same as a 5-in-6 pitch. Your exact center point is at 6 feet over, already marked with a chalk line. Now all you do is measure up from that point 5 feet and that's your peak. Mark it.

Snap a chalk line from the 7-foot 6-inch mark on the edge of the floor to the newly established roof peak point. This will give you an accurate full-scale drawing of the outside edges of your wall. Those measurements are the measurements of the perimeter framing taken from the outside edges.

Now cut the perimeter pieces starting with the full-length (12 foot) bottom plate. Next cut the two tops, or roof, plates of the wall frame. They run from the peak point to the wall height at 7 feet 6 inches. Cut these two pieces, making sure to include the proper angle where they meet at the peak and at the other ends, where they rest on the vertical pieces. Get this angle right off your chalk lines or cheat and recall that Henry and Charlie's had the same roof pitch and this same angle: 40 degrees. Lay

**Gable end wall is ready for siding.**

the roof plate pieces on the full-scale model and trace the inside edge to where it intersects with the wall. This will give you the height and angle of the corner studs.

Measure the distance from that line down to the floor (and again, don't forget to subtract the thickness of the bottom plate) and cut it. Cut a second piece just like this while you are at it, for the other corner stud. Use your skill saw for these cuts, with the table set at the appropriate angle.

With all perimeter pieces cut and ready to go, I like to nail the wall frame together and then set some temporary toenails to hold it square. Then I mark my stud layouts. This is basically a matter of following the plans. On this particular wall, the only thing that interrupted the stud layout was the main entry door. I framed the door in the same manner that we framed Albert's, allowing room for all of the components, including jack studs, king studs, headers, and cripplers.

To get the studs properly measured and marked, I simply snap more chalk lines on the plywood floor, as I just did for the frame pieces. The king studs run all the way to the sloped top plate. Choose a side on which to mark them and then, on the bottom plate, mark the stud points, starting from the closest outside edge of the wall. Transfer those marks to the parallel line you marked earlier at 7 feet 6 inches and along the bottom. Now snap two chalk lines that start accurately at the bottom plate and run through the points you just marked all the way to the sloped top plate. Measure those distances; then, using the same 40-degree angle from the roof pieces, mark and cut. Be careful to remember if you measured the long sides or short sides of the king studs to know how to mark them. Now lay the king studs in and nail away. They should fit snugly and become the starting points for a beautifully square door frame.

## FRAMING THE DOOR

Cut your header the same length as the space between the king studs at the bottom plate. Quite often wood is bowed, so if you were to take that measurement at 6 feet 8 inches, for instance, it might be well off the proper distances as measured at the plate.

Cut your jacks and nail all of the pieces together.

## FILLING IN THE STUDS

Once the door is framed it is time to fill in the remaining studs. We used a two-foot layout. So, starting from the outside and working in, we marked one edge of our stud locations along the bottom plate. Following the same procedure we used to make the king studs, we chalked, measured, marked, and cut the remaining studs.

Once those were nailed in position the wall was ready to sheathe. We used ½-inch CDX plywood. What a pleasure it is to use compared to OSB. Do this the same way we did it at Albert's treehouse.

## TRIMMING AND SIDING

It is time to trim and side the wall. I used tar paper on the walls to protect the framing from the wildly variable Alaska weather conditions. I figured it couldn't hurt, and it is easy to apply with a utility knife and a hammer-type staple gun.

Starting with the trim, I applied temporary casing around the rough opening of the door to approximate as closely as possible where the final casing would be.

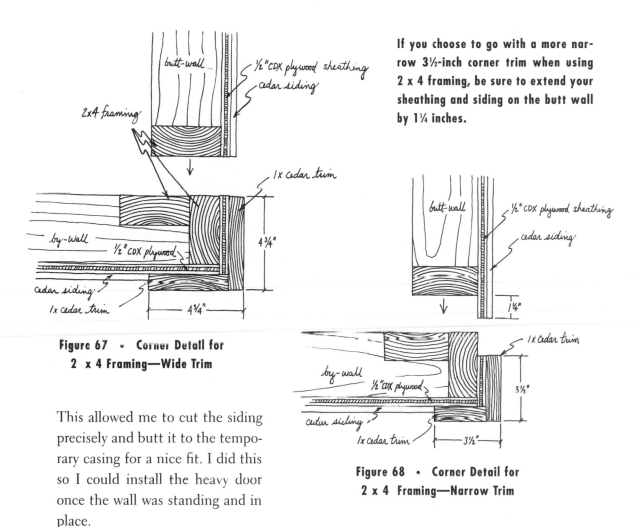

If you choose to go with a more narrow 3½-inch corner trim when using 2 x 4 framing, be sure to extend your sheathing and siding on the butt wall by 1¼ inches.

**Figure 67 • Corner Detail for 2 x 4 Framing—Wide Trim**

**Figure 68 • Corner Detail for 2 x 4 Framing—Narrow Trim**

This allowed me to cut the siding precisely and butt it to the temporary casing for a nice fit. I did this so I could install the heavy door once the wall was standing and in place.

The corner trim detail is much the same as that for the other treehouses. You must remember to add an extra 4 inches of ½-inch sheathing on the end of the frame so it matches up with the next wall that will butt to it.

Now your wall should look complete. Since you need the floor to lay out the next wall, it is time to lift this wall up and nail it in position.

Since this time you used 2 × 4-inch framing, simply snap a chalk line 3½ inches from the edge of the plywood floor along the 12-foot length. When standing in position, the outside edge of the wall should line up flush with the ends of the plywood floor and the chalk line.

Tilt the wall up with the help of at least three people. Once the wall is up, move it into position with a coordinated slide. Be careful not to let the wall get away from you and slip or fall over the edge.

## Framing the Remaining Walls

If you have read this far you will already have all of the basic knowledge you need to frame the remaining walls on your own. Rather than go into detail on each of them, I'm just going to hit the highlights, give some pointers, and explore the tricky parts. Just keep your wits about you.

It's a group effort to tilt up a finished wall.

North wall is on a platform, our only flat surface. When siding's done, wall is ready to tilt up.

### THE NORTH WALL

The second wall—the north wall—has no particularly tricky features. Just remember to extend your sheathing and siding by 1¼ inches if you want your corner trim to be narrower (see corner detail, Figure 68). You will, however, encounter your first window on this wall. We chose to install the windows while the walls were on the ground. This turned out to be a good idea for a few reasons. Let me explain how we went about it.

**The team raises the east wall.**

## INSTALLING WINDOWS

Oddly enough, these windows were left over from the same job from which I obtained my windows for the Fall City treehouse. (I will tell you that story some other time.) Since Gus was on a tight budget, I had them shipped up to Anchorage, where for the $120 shipping cost and a six-hour round-trip car ride to pick them up, Gus was able to assure his place in history as a champion scrounger.

We framed the rough opening in the typical fashion, allowing about $3/8$ to $1/2$ inch of space on all sides. (Have your tar paper already installed. Remember, the wall is still lying on the ground.) To make sure the window was resting at the right height in relation to its casing, we cut 3- or 4-inch blocks of $1/2$-inch plywood to a width of $2\frac{1}{2}$ inches and nailed them to the sides of the rough opening flush with the floor. With the blocks in place we were able to place the windows into the rough openings

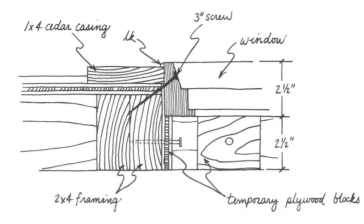

**Figure 69 • Window Installation Detail**

**Inclement weather was no hindrance. We rigged up a rain tarp during a thunderstorm.**

and have them protrude enough to carry the finish casing (a simple nailing flange would have come in handy here, but such is life). We secured the windows using a countersink drill bit and screws. Countersinking is when you drill a hole big enough to allow the head of the screw to fit flush to the work, or even to sink into the work to be covered by dowels, putty, or, in our case, white caulk. Countersink bits can be expensive, but a good one is well worth the price. They help immensely in keeping finish work from splitting.

We used a traditional exterior casing detail on Gus's house. I started each window by cutting and installing the sill piece. This piece helps rain drip away from the window. It was made by ripping a 2-inch-wide board out of a 2 × 4, then putting a 12-degree bevel cut on the last 1¼ inches of the top edge. I cut the sill 9 inches wider than the window so when the 3½-inch (1 × 4) side pieces came down into the sill piece, there remained a 1-inch "ear" on each side. I secured the sill flush with the framing at the base of the window with 16-penny galvanized casing nails. Next I cut the side pieces from 1 × 4 so that it extended flush to the top of the window. I secured these with 10-penny galvanized casing nails and a good bit of silicone caulk along the window edge. Once these were in place, I measured between the outside distances of the side casing and added 2 inches to get the same "ear" detail for the top casing. I cut this out of 1 × 4 as well. Again, it's a good idea to put a good bead of caulk on the edge of the casing where it meets the window. When this piece is secure I go over all of the joints with caulk, including where the casing meets the tar paper.

## THE EAST WALL

The part that makes this east wall a bit tricky is the way the covered porch bites into one of the corners. The bottom plate extends only 10 feet. You also have the slope of the covered porch to build. The framing plan will address any questions on how to build this.

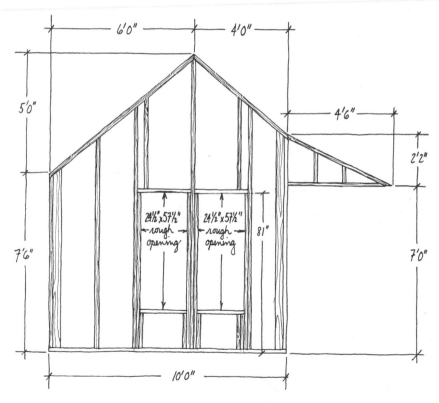

**Figure 70  •  East Wall Framing Plan**

Revisiting Gus's House

In a whirling blur, the last wall was fit into place.

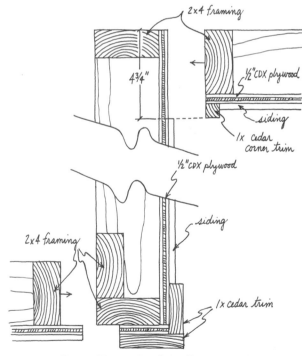

**Figure 71 • South Wall Jog Detail**

## THE SOUTH WALL

The south wall has a 5-foot-wide French door on one end, a 2-foot 90-degree jog, then a long set of kitchen windows on the other end. I built these in three separate components, each to a finished height of 7 feet 6 inches. As with the other windows, I set the bottom of the header 82 inches off the floor. Gus is a tall person, so I tried to keep things at full height. I added an inch to the rough opening height of doors so we would have some room to play with. Figure 71 details the 2-foot jog wall and how it relates to the other two. This will reveal how to measure your plate length and also show the points at which to side and trim.

## The Roof

Gus was extremely easy to work with as we labored over his tiny house. He worked hard alongside us, fed us well, and kept us in beer at night. At least twice a day he would remind us all how lucky we were to be there, at that moment, in Clam Gulch, Alaska, working on a treehouse. He wasn't building his dream house blindly, however, and he took a keen interest in my building methods and techniques. Perhaps my not giving him the time to skin his beams properly on that first day before we hoisted them into position gave him his first cause for concern. My insistence upon using one bolt per connection may have given rise to more concern. The logs we could skin later, I said, both knowing that that time would most likely never come. The one-bolt idea I was able to skirt only with bravado

**Measure twice, cut once.**

and the inflated talk of experience and arboriculture. We were on a tight time schedule. Each time these questions came to Gus he would not hesitate to inquire. It was not hard to detect in him a hint of skepticism of my answers. (He has since backed up the one-bolt with a safety cable.) I am afraid the cat came out of the bag, however, when he showed me the words etched directly on material I used for the

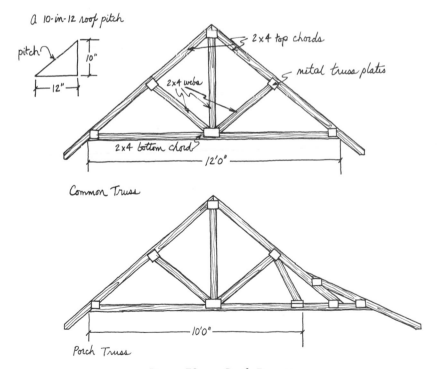

**Figure 72 • Roof Trusses**

**Gus and I install the outriggers that create the roof overhang.**

trusses—as I was pounding in the last nail plate of the first roof truss: "DO NOT USE FOR ROOF TRUSSES." Not having noticed the inscription until that moment, I could only smile and change the subject. What the hell else were you supposed to use them for?

Trusses are prefabricated roof components that do all of the work of roof rafters but use smaller dimensioned material. You can build them from 2 × 4s on the ground and easily hoist them into position. They are easy to build and versatile. The secret that makes the truss work is that of the mighty triangle. That was a principle I had not yet grasped when I built the trusses for Gus's house. I have since revised the design and it now appears as it should in Figure 72.

And don't forget to use proper nail plates! These are metal plates of different sizes that have a multitude of sharp points stamped out at 90 degrees from the plate's face. They are commonly used at all of the various connections found in

**The crack crew gives me a chance to ponder our next steps.**

trusses and, if properly installed, create a very strong bond. I have seen the same principle applied using ½-inch CDX plywood gussets to sandwich the same connection points, nailed liberally with 8-penny nails.

You'll need to build two types of trusses. Make four simple trusses and three extended trusses for the covered porch area. The end rafters, outriggers, and barge rafters use the same detail described for Albert's treehouse.

Cut your frieze blocks, mark your top plates, and start nailing. Begin with the end rafters on the west wall. Notch for the outriggers on the ground but run the outriggers themselves long off the west face. Nail the frieze blocks on the top of both walls at the beginning of the run, then set the first simple truss into position and nail it home. Go back to your outriggers and snap a chalk line 10½ inches out from the end rafter. This will insure a straight cut for your barge rafter to butt against. Rather than using a 2 × 4 barge rafter, we chose to beef it up by using a heavy 2 × 8.

**With roof sheathing in place, it's time to roll tar paper and attach composition roofing.**

Mark the appropriate plumb cuts at the peak and tail of the barge rafters, then put them in position and send them home with a few 16-penny galvanized casing nails per outrigger.

Now move across the roof and nail in the remaining frieze blocks and trusses. To keep the peaks from falling over as you progress across the roof, nail a long 2 × 4 to the end rafter at the peak. As you nail in your trusses, nail the peak at its proper spacing to the 2 × 4 brace. This brace plays an important role in keeping your trusses in line. It can stay there until you're ready to cover it with the roof sheathing.

The extended porch trusses begin 9 feet in from the west wall. I spaced the remaining trusses evenly across to the east end rafter. Use the same outrigger detail on the end rafter. This time you'll need to cut short the south sloping barge rafter to accommodate the extended porch. To provide adequate support for the two pieces on that slope, set two outriggers per section.

Now sheathe the roof. Start at the west end of the south pitch and nail ½-inch CDX directly to the base of the trusses using 8-penny nails spaced every 10 inches or so. The transition of the main roof pitch to the porch roof pitch is the only part of the roof that needs further explanation.

I nailed a ledger block on the west side of the first extended truss that maintains the same roof pitch, so the plywood sheathing could run all the way to the side of this truss. I applied a short barge rafter that accommodates the west porch roof overhang after the first row of sheathing was nailed in place. I cut in two outriggers for this barge rafter so that it could be kept off the roof sheathing by about 1½ inches. This way, we could slip tar paper and roofing under the barge rafter, insuring a nice watertight seal.

Nail off the remaining sheathing and start rolling tar paper. We used cheap asphalt 3-tab composition on Gus's treehouse just as we did at the World Treehouse Headquarters. Since Gus was rapidly developing his Martha Stewart side, he chose a delightful green-colored roofing, which, I must admit, matched up quite nicely with the white window trim and natural cedar siding.

## Interior trim

The level of finish that Gus was willing or able to accept inside his treehouse was a question that was plaguing me all project long. I knew we were getting close to the end of his fishing reserves, so I was pleasantly surprised when he pulled up at just the right time with a pickup full of 1 × 6-inch tongue-and-groove paneling. We saved some money by using ½-inch ACX plywood on the ceiling only. We paneled the rest of the walls the same way we paneled Albert's home.

We saved time and money by using ACX plywood on the ceiling instead of the 1x6 tongue-and-groove paneling that we put on the wall.

We started by hanging the ACX plywood on the ceiling. To access the attic space, we boxed between two trusses and created an opening about 2 feet square. This access hole enabled us to insulate the ceiling by rolling out R-30 batts of fiberglass insulation directly on top of it, just as we had in Fall City.

We used R-11 kraft-backed fiberglass insulation in all the exterior walls. I recommend a hammer stapler to apply this. Don't forget to wear a good dust mask and gloves when installing fiberglass insulation.

We paneled just as we did at Albert's. The only difference here was that we set the windows 2½ inches in from the edge of the framing. So we had to build a sec-

**A myriad of last-minute details fill the final day of the project. Remember to bank extra time for the unexpected.**

ondary window jamb to fill that distance and give us something to nail our casing to. I built these boxes in the same way I built the jambs for Charlie and Henry's treehouse. I made them from 1 × 4-inch cedar ripped to 3¼ inches so that it would stick out ¾ inch from the framing and line up flush with the ¾-inch wall paneling. I nailed the jamb through all four faces into the framing with 2-inch finish nails. Shims held the jamb square in place while I nailed.

Next I marked a ¼-inch reveal around the jamb. Once that line is drawn on all four sides, you can choose whatever kind of casing you want. Just be sure to line it up flush with the reveal.

## Final Details

There were some final important details we needed to add to Gus's treehouse to make it a home. The most crucial, life-or-death detail was finding a good heat source.

Luckily, Gus had gotten his hands on a compact woodstove from a fellow dog musher a few weeks before the project began. It took up a good bit of room, but sacrificing space for warmth has been well worth it. Periodic word from Gus confirms he is still alive.

We vented the stove out the side wall, which later proved to be a mistake because it didn't draw very well. Gus revented it through the roof this spring and it's working much better.

Gus also needed a place to lay his head. We thought a built-in bed would be a nice touch. We designed storage space underneath and bookshelves in the front 12 inches. This became the architectural focal point of the interior design. Unfortunately, after the whole thing was completed, Gus discovered the bed was a few agonizing inches too short. On one fateful night last January Gus took care of the problem with his trusty chain saw.

Heating, a bed . . . what was left to make Gus's home complete? A kitchen. So, along the front side of his house, we built an 8-foot-long, 2-foot-wide countertop meant for a sink and a countertop stove of some kind.

Finally, an Adirondack deck railing seemed the perfect complement to Gus's rustic retreat. Katie, John's wife, created this small piece of art, fashioning it from birch boughs. We attached it to the porch as we did at Albert's treehouse.

**East wall of Gus's finished home.**

By the time I had to pack up and leave, Gus was already moving his stuff in.

Looking at Gus's new treehome, for a moment I felt as if I could actually live in Alaska too. So what if it's freezing and rainy a lot and dark most of the year? That's not terribly different than Seattle, after all. Gus sure had himself a great new place to live.

That's what it's all about, I thought. You wake up in the morning to the smell of cut timber and wool blankets. The residual heat of your woodstove reaches out and wraps itself around you. Your eyes adjust slowly to the slanted morning light. Waking up like this is easy. You don't fight it. You stand up and stretch and glance out your window and are reminded. The most simple joy washes over you. Oh yeah, that's right—you're in a tree.

**Gus Gunther has a place to call his own.**

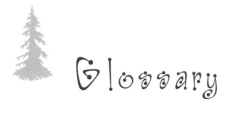

# Glossary

**Adze**: a hatchetlike tool used to flatten wood surfaces.

**Arborist**: a tree-care expert and invaluable resource.

**Arresting chain**: a safety mechanism used in conjunction with the floating point load foundation system.

**Barge boards**: the finishing boards that attach to the ends of a gabled roof.

**Barge rafter**: the outermost rafter of a gabled roof.

**Beam**: a horizontal structural element in construction upon which floor or deck joists, or roof rafters, rest. Beams are supported by walls or posts.

**Bevel square**: an adjustable tool used to measure and hold any angle.

**Blocking**: framing elements used often between studs and floor joists to help strengthen walls and floors, and to slow fires from rising.

**Bottom plate**: the framing member that runs the length of a wall at its base.

**Bowline knot**: a simple knot that can take a lot of weight or stress but unties easily.

**Butt-wall**: wall that is contained on both sides by the by-walls.

**By-wall**: wall that runs past butt-walls.

**Carabiner**: a metal loop, typically used by rock climbers, that opens and closes to hold lines.

**Ceiling joist**: the horizontal framing member that rests on the top plate of a wall and spans from one wall to another.

**Chalk line**: a marking device that uses string and chalk to mark straight lines.

**Chop saw**: a circular saw mounted on an adjustable bracket that allows for plunging cuts.

**Climber's knot**: a self-hoisting friction knot commonly used by arborists.

**Combination square**: a small adjustable square used to mark ninety-degree lines for cuts or reveals.

**Come along**: a winchlike tool used to move or lift heavy objects.

**Common rafter**: the framing members that support the roof.

**Common studs**: the vertical framing members used in an ordinary wall layout.

**Corner studs**: the vertical framing members at the ends of a wall.

**Corner trim**: the finish material used on the exterior corners of a house.

**Crippler**: the framing member that supports the sill of a window's rough frame.

**Door casing**: the trim material that wraps around the sides and top of a door.

**Draw knife**: a straight blade about 12 to 16 inches in width with a handle on each end, used to take bark off trees.

**Fixed point load**: a rigid bolt connection between a wooden beam and a tree.

**Flashing**: strips of thin metal usually applied under roofing and siding to repel water from walls and windows.

**Floating point load**: a connection between a beam and a tree that allows a certain amount of movement for both the beam and the tree to which it is connected.

**Floor joist**: a structural framing member that typically runs on edge and supports the floor. Joists in turn are supported by beams or walls.

**Flush**: even with one another.

**Framing square**: a tool used to square small areas and cut stair stringers and roof rafters.

**Gable**: the pointed end of a building that is created by the meeting of two roof planes.

**Hauling lines**: lines used to lift materials and tools to a desired location.

**Header**: the framing member placed above doors and windows that is used to support the extra downward forces created by a break in the standard spacing of the studs.

**Hip rafter**: the roof rafter created where two roof planes come together, and where that is not considered a peak or a ridge.

**Impact wrench**: a power tool used to drive or loosen bolts or nuts.

**Jack rafter**: a roof framing member that joins to a hip rafter and supports the roof.

**Jack stud**: the framing member used in conjunction with a king stud to support a header.

**Jamb**: the vertical frame of a door or a window.

**King stud**: a framing member used in conjunction with a jack stud to support a window or door header.

**Knee brace**: a support post that angles back and below from the beam it supports to the trunk of the tree.

**Lag bolt**: a large screw with a square head.

**Lanyard**: a safety rope used when securing oneself above the ground.

**On edge**: position of a piece of lumber when it supports a weight on its narrow side.

**Outriggers**: the framing members that span outside the exterior wall line to support a building's eave and barge rafter.

**Pitch**: the slope of a roof.

**Plumb**: level in the vertical plane.

**Plumb line**: a tool that has a tear drop-shaped weight at the end of a string used to find the level on the vertical plane.

**Posting down**: using a post to support a horizontal span of a beam.

**Prusik knot**: a friction knot made by creating a series of loops around a line that tighten when weight is applied.

**Reveal**: the amount of a piece of wood left visible by another overlapping piece of wood.

**Ridge cap**: the uppermost part of roofing that covers the roof ridge.

**Rim joist**: joist that caps the ends of the common joists on both sides.

**Roof trusses**: prefabricated roof supports that sit on the top plate of a wall or on a beam.

**Scribing**: process of marking and cutting wood to accommodate an irregularly shaped intrusion, such as the trunk of the tree or its branches.

**Sheathing**: the wood, typically plywood, used as an under-layment to siding or roofing. It is applied directly to the frame of the structure.

**Shim**: a thin, wedge-shaped piece of wood, typically cedar, used in a door or window jamb to create a flat and nailable spacer.

**Sill**: a horizontal framing member at the base of a window's rough framing.

**Skip sheathing**: a method of roofing or siding that uses alternating rows of sheathing and open spaces.

**Sliding slot**: a method of attaching a beam to a tree in which the main bolt(s) slide in a horizontal slot, giving the beam and tree some flexibility.

**Spacers**: short sections of galvanized pipe that thread over bolts and hold beams away from trees so trees have room to grow.

**Speed square**: an essential carpentry tool that allows quick ninety- and forty-five-degree markings on framing lumber.

**Stringers**: the sides of a stair upon which the treads and risers rest.

**Suspended point load**: a method of attachment where the beams are suspended by cables.

**Top plate**: the framing member that runs the length of the wall along the top.

**Tree-grip dead end**: a preformed cable splicer that creates a strong loop at the end of the cable.

**Umbrella foundation**: a style of framework used in building in one tree without posting down to ground. The beams together form an umbrella pattern, with the tree at the center.

**Wainscoting**: the lower segment of an interior wall that differs from the rest of the wall.

**Wind shear**: the force on a building created by wind.

**Window casing**: the trim used around the interior and exterior of a window.

# Resources

## SUPPLIERS:

AMERICAN ARBORIST SUPPLIES, INC.
882 South Matlack St.
West Chester, PA 19382
610-430-1214
800-441-8381

P.J. PLAYHOUSE, INC.
P.O. Box 1136
Fall City, WA 98024
800-248-8520

THE REAL GOODS COMPANY
555 Leslie St.
Ukiah, CA 95482
800-762-7325

RESOURCE WOODWORKS, INC.
627 East 60th St.
Tacoma, WA 98404
206-474-3757
*(Al Baker)*

TERRY'S SHAKE AND SHINGLE
22310 SR 530 NE
Arlington, WA 98223
360-435-2081
*(Terry Blacker)*

TWO RIVERS WINDOW COMPANY
17703 15th Ave. NE
Shoreline, WA 98155
206-363-8136
*(Kevin Sweeters)*

## SERVICES AND ORGANIZATIONS:

ARBORVITAE TREE CARE
608 Glenridge Rd.
Glenmore, PA 19343
610-458-9756
*(Jonathan Fairoaks)*

CALIFORNIA ANCIENT FOREST ADVEN-
TURES
P. O. Box 703
Arcata, CA 95518
916-623-3300
*(Doug Thron)*

OUT 'N' ABOUT TREEHOUSE TREESORT
300 Page Creek Rd.
Cave Junction, OR 97523
541-592-2208
800-200-5484
*(Michael Garnier)*

THE TARZAN HOUSE
Ariau Jungle Lodge
Amazonas, Brazil
805-688-8646

TREEHOUSE LODGE AT KHAO SOK
NATIONAL PARK, THAILAND
c/o Asia Transpacific Journeys
3055 Center Green Drive
Boulder, CO 80301
303-443-6789
800-642-2742
*(Eric Kareus)*

WAIPI'O TREE HOUSE
P. O. Box 5086
Hono Kaa, Hawaii 96727
808-775-7160
*(Linda Peach)*

WORLD TREEHOUSE ASSOCIATION
(W.T.A.)
32617 SE 44th St.
Fall City, WA 98024
206-222-7881
worldtreehouse.com
*Tee shirts & annual meetings in October;*
*Treehouse info & exchanges*

# Further Reading

Christopher Alexander, *A Pattern Language* (New York: Oxford University Press, 1977).

Mario Bigon and Guido Regazzoni, *The Morrow Guide to Knots* (New York: William Morrow and Co., 1982).

Marie-France Boyer, *Cabin Fever* (London: Thames and Hudson, Inc., 1993).

Italo Calvino, *The Baron in the Trees* (New York: Harcourt Brace & Co., 1957).

"Frame Carpentry," *Fine Homebuilding* (Newtown, CT: Taunton Press, 1990).

"Framing Roofs," *Fine Homebuilding* (Newtown, CT: Taunton Press, 1996).

S. J. Lilly, *The Tree Worker's Manual* (Columbus, OH: Ohio Agricultural Education Curriculum Materials Service, 1992).

Peter Nelson, *Treehouses, the Art and Craft of Living Out on a Limb* (Boston: Houghton Mifflin Co., 1994).

David Pearson, *The Natural House Book* (New York: Simon & Schuster, Inc., 1989).

Roger Phillips, *Trees of North America and Europe* (New York: Random House, 1978).

John Shaeffer and The Real Goods Staff, *Solar Living Sourcebook: The Complete Guide to Renewable Energy Technologies & Sustainable Living* (White River Junction, VT: Chelsea Green Publishing, 1996).

Alex L. Shigo, *100 Tree Myths* (Durham, NH: Shigo and Trees, Associates, 1993).

"Tips and Techniques for Builders," *Fine Homebuilding* (Newtown, CT: Taunton Press, 1988).

# Supply Lists

## Kid's Treehouse Materials List

STRUCTURAL FRAMEWORK AND FLOOR

> (5) 2" × 4" × 8' (pressure treated)
> (1) ⅝" × 4' × 8' CDX plywood

WALL FRAMES

> (20) 2" × 2" × 8'
> (42) 1" × 2" × 8'

EXTERIOR SIDING AND TRIM

> (4) 1" × 8" × 8' cedar
> (12) 1" × 4" × 8' cedar
> (2) 2" × 4" × 8' cedar
> (1) ¾ squares #1 western red cedar shingles

ROOF

> (23) 1" × 2" × 8'
> (1) ¾ squares #1 western red cedar shingles

WINDOWS

(2) 24" × 29"
(2) 23" × 36"

HARDWARE

(5) pair of 3" hinges

2 lbs. 3" self-tapping wood screws

5 lbs. 16-penny finish nails

3 lbs. 7-penny galvanized siding nails

3 lbs. 4-penny galvanized siding nails

34" x 1½" wide 26-gauge flashing

½" lag screws with washers—check situation for lengths and quantity

½" galvanized nipple spacers—check situation for lengths and quantity

## Albert's Montana Treehouse Materials List

STRUCTURAL FRAMEWORK

(4) 4" × 8" × 8' pressure-treated (beams)

(4) 4" × 8" × 10' pressure-treated (beams)

(4) 4" × 8" × 12' pressure-treated (knee braces)

FLOOR FRAME AND CEDAR DECKING

(9) 2" × 6" × 14' (floor joists)

(6) 2" × 6" × 8' (floor blocking)

(5) ¾" tongue-and-groove CDX plywood (interior subfloors)

(5) 2" × 6" × 10' cedar (entry deck)

(15) 2" × 6" × 8' cedar (main deck)

Supply Lists

## WALL FRAMES

(7) 2" × 4" × 8' (headers)

(2) 2" × 2" × 12' (wall—6 plates)

(12) 2" × 2" × 10' (studs)

(92) 2" × 2" × 8' (studs, plates, and blocking)

(12) ½" × 4' × 8' CDX plywood (sheathing)

## EXTERIOR SIDING AND TRIM

3 squares No. 1 or No. 2 cedar shingles

(20) ⁵⁄₄" × 4" × 8' cedar (window, door, and corner casing)

(8) ⁵⁄₄" × 6" × 8' cedar (window casing)

## ROOF

(12) 2" × 4" × 10' (rafters)

(14) 2" × 4" × 8' (rafters and blocking)

440 linear feet 1" × 6" pine tongue and groove (sheathing)

1 roll (300 square feet) of 15 lb. roofing felt

(22) 1" × 2" × 8' (roof sleepers)

220 square feet roofing material

## WINDOWS AND DOORS

(2) 2'6" × 6'8" prehung glass doors

(2) 18" × 18" picture window

(2) 18" × 30" picture window

(1) 18" × 36" picture window

(1) 36" × 60" picture window

(1) 18" × 42" picture window

(1) 42" × 42" picture window

(1) 36" × 65" bay window

(2) 9" × 65" bay window

INTERIOR PANELING, CASING, AND FLOORS

600 linear foot 1" × 6" pine tongue and groove (paneling)

300 linear foot 1" × 4" cedar (casing)

350 linear foot 1" × 6" pine boards (flooring)

HARDWARE

(8) upper brackets

(8) lower brackets

(8) angle brackets

(16) ¾" × 8" galvanized lag screws w/ washers

(24) ⅝" × 3" galvanized lag screws w/ washers

(32) ⅝" × 4 ½" galvanized machine bolts w/ locking washers

25 lbs. 16-penny sinker nails

20 lbs. 16-penny finish nails

15 lbs. 8-penny ring shank nails

10 lbs. 12-penny galvanized deck nails

8 lbs. 7-penny galvanized siding nails

10 lbs. 5-penny galvanized shingle nails

8 lbs. 10-penny galvanized casing nails

20 lbs. 8-penny finish nails

3 lbs. 3" self-tapping wood screws

## Fall City Treehouse Materials List

STRUCTURAL FRAMEWORK

    (2) 4" × 12" × 22' (beams)

    (1) 4" × 12" × 12' (entry beam)

FLOOR FRAME AND CEDAR DECKING

    (9) $2\frac{5}{8}$" × 13" × 16' (floor joists)

    (5) $2\frac{5}{8}$" × 13" × 8' (entry joists)

    (8) $\frac{3}{4}$" × 4' × 8' tongue-and-groove CDX plywood (interior subfloor)

    (15) $\frac{5}{4}$" × 4" × 8' cedar decking (entry porch)

WALL FRAMES AND PORCH FRAME

    (80) 2" × 2" × 8' (stud plates)

    (1) 2" × 4" × 10' (west wall header)

    (3) 2" × 4" × 8' (headers)

    700 linear feet 1" × 2" × 8' (skip sheathing)

    (2) 2" × 6" × 8' (porch headers)

    (1) 4" × 4" × 8' (porch post)

EXTERIOR SIDING, TRIM, PORCH POST, AND RAILING

    (3.5) squares No. 1 or No. 2 cedar shingles

    (25) $\frac{5}{4}$" × 4" × 8' cedar (window casing and corner trim)

    (12) $\frac{5}{4}$" × 6" × 8' cedar (window top casing and skirt boards)

    (8) 2" × 4" × 8' cedar (drip edge)

    (8) 1" × 6" × 8' cedar (skirt boards)

    (8) 1" × 8" × 8' cedar (soffit boards)

    (4) 1" × 8" × 8' cedar (porch post surround)

(9) 2" × 2" × 8' cedar (railing balusters)

(2) ⁵⁄₄" × 4" × 8' cedar (railing top and bottom subcaps)

(4) 2" × 4" × 8' cedar (rail top and bottom caps)

ROOF

(4) 2" × 6" × 16' (hip rafters)

(4) 2" × 6" × 10' (common rafters)

(12) 2" × 6" × 8' (jack rafters)

(8) 2" × 6" × 16' (ceiling joists)

(12) ½" × 4' × 8' CDX plywood (sheathing)

2 rolls 15 lb. roofing felt

375 square feet roofing material

WINDOWS AND DOORS

(1) 2'8" × 6'8 ½" light entry door

(1) 2'6" × 6'8" glass door

(3) 33" × 57" top vented windows

(2) 33" × 39" top vented windows

(1) 21" × 44" picture window

INSULATION

220 square feet R-30 insulation (ceiling)

(20) 2' × 8" × 1½" rigid foam insulation (walls)

220 square feet R-19 insulation (floor)

(8) ⅜" × 4' × 8' T-111 plywood (insulation cover under floor)

(32) 1" × 2" × 8' (nailers for plywood insulation covers)

## INTERIOR PANELING, CASING, AND FLOORS

1200 linear feet 1" × 6" shiplap paneling (walls and ceiling)

300 linear feet window and door casing and chair rail

200 square feet 1" × 3" tongue-and-groove fir flooring

1 roll vapor barrier (between subfloor and finish floor)

## HARDWARE

(4) ¾" × 12" galvanized lag screws w/ washers

(4) ⅝" drop forged eye-lags w/ thimbles (backup cable)

20 feet ⅜" EHS cable

(8) ⅜" Tree-Grip dead-ends

(4) 2' ⅝" galvanized chain lengths

20 lbs. 6" pole barn nails (joist nails)

25 lbs. 16-penny sinker nails

20 lbs. 16-penny finish nails

15 lbs. 8-penny ring shank nails

10 lbs. 12-penny galvanized deck nails

8 lbs. 7-penny galvanized siding nails

10 lbs. 5-penny galvanized shingle nails

8 lbs. 10-penny galvanized casing nails

20 lbs. 8-penny finish nails

3 lbs. 3" self-tapping wood screws

## Gus's Alaska Treehouse Material List

### STRUCTURAL FRAMEWORK

(4) 6" x 8" × 24' log beams

(3) 6" x 8" × 8' log posts

(1) 2" × 10" × 20' (rim joist)

## FLOOR FRAME AND CEDAR DECKING

(6) 2" × 10" × 16' (floor joists)

(8) 2" × 10" × 12' (floor joists and floor blocking)

(6) ¾" × 4' × 8' tongue-and-groove CDX plywood (interior subfloor)

(20) 2" × 6" × 8' cedar (decking)

## WALL FRAMES

(2) 2" × 4" × 16' (north wall plates)

(1) 2" × 4" × 14' (stud)

(5) 2" × 4" × 12' (studs and plates)

(10) 2" × 4" × 10' (studs and plates)

(65) 2" × 4" × 8' (studs and plates)

(1) 2" × 6" × 10' (kitchen header)

(3) 2" × 6" × 8' (headers)

(16) ½" × 4' × 8' CDX plywood (sheathing)

## EXTERIOR SIDING AND TRIM

350 square feet cedar bevel siding

2 rolls side-wall building paper

(36) 1" × 4" × 8' cedar (corner and window trim)

(7) 2" × 4" × 8' cedar (windowsill casing and drip edge)

## ROOF

(4) 2" × 4" × 14' truss (bottom chord porch truss)

(5) 2" × 4" × 12' truss (bottom chord bottom truss)

(15) 2" × 4" × 10' truss (top chords)

(30) 2" × 4" × 8' truss (top chords and webs)

(12) ½" × 4' × 8' CDX plywood (sheathing)

400 square feet roofing paper

400 square feet roofing material

WINDOWS AND DOORS

(1) 5'0" × 6'8" glass French door

(1) 3'0" × 6'8" entry door

(2) 24" × 57" top vented windows

(1) 18" × 18" venting window

(1) 57" × 36" picture window

(1) 52" × 36" picture window

(2) 20" × 36" venting window

INSULATION

400 square feet R-30 insulation (roof and floor)

300 square feet R-11 insulation (walls)

(6) ⅜" × 4' × 8' T-111 plywood (insulation cover under floor joists)

INTERIOR FRAMING, PANELING, AND CASING

(8) 2" × 4" × 8' (closet framing)

(10) 2" × 4" × 8' (bed framing)

(2) ¾" × 4' × 8' CDX plywood (bed surface and kitchen countertop)

(10) 2" × 2" × 8' (kitchen cabinet framing)

1200 linear feet 1" × 6" pine tongue-and-groove paneling (walls and ceiling)

300 linear feet 1" × 4" cedar (casing materials)

## HARDWARE

(4) ¾" × 14" galvanized lag screws w/ washers

15 lbs. 20-penny galvanized nails (joist nails)

25 lbs. 16-penny sinker nails

20 lbs. 16-penny finish nails

(4) ⅝" drop-forged eye-lags w/ thimbles (backup cable)

20 feet ⅜" EHS cable

(8) ⅜" Tree-Grip dead-ends

(4) 2 foot ⅝" galvanized chain lengths

15 lbs. 8-penny ring shank nails

10 lbs. 12-penny galvanized deck nails

15 lbs. 7-penny galvanized siding nails

8 lbs. 10-penny galvanized casing nails

20 lbs. 8-penny finish nails

3 lbs. 3" self-tapping wood screws

Treehouses are not meant to last forever, but they are not meant to be dangerous either. Be sure to inspect all posts and beams for signs of rot or deep cracks, particularly if you are using salvaged materials. This disaster happened as a result of a rotted main support post and high winds. Make sure this doesn't happen to you!

## FOR THE BEST IN PAPERBACKS, LOOK FOR THE

In every corner of the world, on every subject under the sun, Penguin represents quality and variety—the very best in publishing today.

For complete information about books available from Penguin—including Puffins, Penguin Classics, and Arkana—and how to order them, write to us at the appropriate address below. Please note that for copyright reasons the selection of books varies from country to country.

**In the United Kingdom:** Please write to *Dept. JC, Penguin Books Ltd, FREEPOST, West Drayton, Middlesex UB7 0BR.*

If you have any difficulty in obtaining a title,.please send your order with the correct money, plus ten percent for postage and packaging, to *P.O. Box No. 11, West Drayton, Middlesex UB7 0BR*

**In the United States:** Please write to *Consumer Sales, Penguin USA, P.O. Box 999, Dept. 17109, Bergenfield, New Jersey 07621-0120.* VISA and MasterCard holders call 1-800-253-6476 to order all Penguin titles

**In Canada:** Please write to *Penguin Books Canada Ltd, 10 Alcorn Avenue, Suite 300, Toronto, Ontario M4V 3B2*

**In Australia:** Please write to *Penguin Books Australia Ltd, P.O. Box 257, Ringwood, Victoria 3134*

**In New Zealand:** Please write to *Penguin Books (NZ) Ltd, Private Bag 102902, North Shore Mail Centre, Auckland 10*

**In India:** Please write to *Penguin Books India Pvt Ltd, 706 Eros Apartments, 56 Nehru Place, New Delhi 110 019*

**In the Netherlands:** Please write to *Penguin Books Netherlands bv, Postbus 3507, NL-1001 AH Amsterdam*

**In Germany:** Please write to *Penguin Books Deutschland GmbH, Metzlerstrasse 26, 60594 Frankfurt am Main*

**In Spain:** Please write to *Penguin Books S. A., Bravo Murillo 19, 1° B, 28015 Madrid*

**In Italy:** Please write to *Penguin Italia s.r.l., Via Felice Casati 20, I-20124 Milano*

**In France:** Please write to *Penguin France S. A., 17 rue Lejeune, F—31000 Toulouse*

**In Japan:** Please write to *Penguin Books Japan, Ishikiribashi Building, 2–5–4, Suido, Bunkyo-ku, Tokyo 112*

**In Greece:** Please write to *Penguin Hellas Ltd, Dimocritou 3, GR–106 71 Athens*

**In South Africa:** Please write to *Longman Penguin Southern Africa (Pty) Ltd, Private Bag X08, Bertsham 2013*